Upland Autumn

Also by William G. Tapply

Brady Coyne Mystery Novels
Death at Charity's Point, Scribner, 1984
The Dutch Blue Error, Scribner, 1985
Follow the Sharks, Scribner, 1985
The Marine Corpse, Scribner 1986
Dead Meat, Scribner, 1987
The Vulgar Boatman, Scribner, 1987
A Void in Hearts, Scribner, 1988
Dead Winter, Delacorte, 1989
Client Privilege, Delacorte, 1989
The Spotted Cats, Delacorte, 1991
Tight Lines, Delacorte, 1992
The Snake Eater, Otto Penzler Books, 1993
The Seventh Enemy, Otto Penzler Books, 1995
Close to the Bone, St. Martin's Press, 1996
Cutter's Run, St. Martin's Press, 1998
Muscle Memory, St. Martin's Press, 1999
Scar Tissue, St. Martin's Press, 2000
Past Tense, St. Martin's Press, 2001
A Fine Line, St. Martin's Press, 2002
Shadow of Death, St. Martin's Press, 2003
Nervous Water, St. Martin's Press, 2005
Out Cold, St. Martin's Press, 2006
One Way Ticket, St. Martin's Press, 2007
Hell Bent, Minotaur, 2008

Stoney Calhoun Mystery Novels
Bitch Creek, The Lyons Press, 2004
Gray Ghost, St. Martin's Press, 2007
Dark Tiger, Minotaur, 2009

Brady Coyne/J.W. Jackson Mystery Novels
First Light, St. Martin's Press, 2001
Second Sight, St. Martin's Press, 2004
Third Strike, St. Martin's Press, 2007

Nonfiction
Those Hours Spent Outdoors, Scribner, 1988
Opening Day and Other Neuroses, Lyons and Burford, 1990
Home Water Near and Far, Lyons and Burford, 1992
Sportsman's Legacy, Lyons and Burford, 1993
A Fly-fishing Life, The Lyons Press, 1997
Bass Bug Fishing, The Lyons Press, 1999
Upland Days, The Lyons Press, 2000
Pocket Water, The Lyons Press, 2001
The Orvis Pocket Guide to Fly Fishing for Bass, The Lyons Press, 2001
Gone Fishin', The Lyons Press, 2004
Trout Eyes, Skyhorse Publishing, 2007

Other Works
The Elements of Mystery Fiction, The Writer, Inc., 1995 and Poisoned Pen Press, 2004
Thicker Than Water, Signet, 1995
A Brady Coyne Omnibus, St. Martin's, 2000
Tap's Tips, Introduction, The Lyons Press, 2004

Upland Autumn

BIRDS, DOGS, AND SHOTGUN SHELLS

William G. Tapply

Skyhorse Publishing

Skyhorse Publishing books may be purchased in bulk at special discounts for sales promotion, corporate gifts, fund-raising, or educational purposes. Special editions can also be created to specifications. For details, contact the Special Sales Department, Skyhorse Publishing, 555 Eighth Avenue, Suite 903, New York, NY 10018 or info@skyhorsepublishing.com.

www.skyhorsepublishing.com

10 9 8 7 6 5 4 3 2 1

Library of Congress Cataloging-in-Publication Data

Tapply, William G.
  Upland autumn : birds, dogs, and shotgun shells / William G. Tapply.
    p. cm.
  ISBN 978-1-60239-783-5 (alk. paper)
  1. Fowling--Northeastern States--Anecdotes. 2. Tapply, William G.--Homes and haunts. I. Title.
  SK313.T36 2009
  799.2'4--dc22

                                        2009024309

Printed in the United States of America

DEDICATION

This book is for my bird-hunting companions . . .
Rick Boyer
Tony Brown
Marty Connolly
Art Currier
Skip Rood
Jason Terry
Keith Wegener
. . . with thanks for all the stories

CONTENTS

ACKNOWLEDGMENTS

I had the rare good luck to have a bird-hunting, outdoor-writing father, H. G. "Tap" Tapply, who for 35 years wrote the "Tap's Tips" and "Sportsman's Notebook" columns for *Field & Stream*. Dad claimed that his job required him to hunt and fish whenever possible, and he took his job seriously. And lucky me, he wouldn't think of going into the woods without inviting his son to tag along—to help with his research, he said.

Most of the men Dad (and I) hunted with were also writers, among them some of the most eminent of their era: Burton L. Spiller, Gorham Cross, Corey Ford, Frank Woolner, Lee Wulff, Ed Zern, and Harold Blaisdell. These men, like my father, hunted for stories as well as for grouse and woodcock. Conversations in the car on the way to and from a day of bird hunting, and in hotel lobbies and at breakfast tables and around campfires, were always literate and witty, bound to rub off on an impressionable kid. I was, I know, fortunate to be shaped by my environment, both as an outdoors person and as an outdoor writer. The spirit that pervades this book harkens back to those days when I walked the upland autumns with those men, and it reflects the values and philosophies of my old mentors.

Most of these stories and essays were previously published in *Field & Stream, Shooting Sportsman, Gray's Sporting Journal,* or *Upland Almanac,* and they all benefited from the scrutiny of these publications' excellent editors: Slaton White, Ralph Stuart, James Babb, and Nancy Ainsfield.

This is an appropriate place for me to say good-bye to Burt, my Brittany, who was my bird-hunting companion for 13 memorable upland autumns. Vicki and I had to put the old boy to rest on December 3, 2008, after a lifetime of mostly spectacular—although occasionally incomprehensible—bird work. Burt always blessed us with his expressive affection, his constant companionship, his unquestioned loyalty, and his joyous playfulness. His spirit ghosts through all of these pages, quick and thorough, the way he worked a woodcock cover. He is and forever will be missed.

Chickadee Farm
Hancock, New Hampshire
January 2009

WHY I HUNT

I hunt because my father hunted, and he took me with him, and we built a bond that has endured past his death, and because his father hunted, and his father's father, and all of the fathers in my line and yours, as far back as those fathers who invented spears and axes and recorded their adventures with pictures on the walls of caves.

I hunt because it links me with the boy I used to be and with the young man my father was then.

I hunt because it keeps my passions alive, my memories fresh, and my senses alert even as my beard grows gray, and because I fear that if I stopped hunting I would become an old man, and because I believe that as long as I hunt I will remain young.

I hunt because I don't buy futures, sell cars, swing deals, negotiate hostile takeovers, or litigate, prosecute, or plea bargain, but because I am nevertheless, like everyone else, a predator. So I go to the woods where I belong.

I hunt because I love ruffed grouse, woodcock, pheasants, quail, and ducks, and because I can imagine no more honorable way for them to die than at the hands of a respectful hunter. As Thoreau understood, ". . . the hunter is the greatest friend of the animals hunted, not excepting the Humane Society."

I hunt because the goldenrod and milkweed glisten when the early morning autumn sun melts the frost from the fields; because native brook trout spawn in hidden October brooks; and because New England uplands glow crimson, orange, and gold in the season of bird hunting.

I hunt because when I stumble upon overgrown cellarholes and family graveyards deep in the woods, it reminds me that I'm connected to the farmers who cleared the land and grew their crops and buried their wives and children there, and who in the process created ideal grouse and woodcock habitat, and because I like to believe that I am the first man in a century to stand in those places.

I hunt because Burton Spiller and Gorham Cross hunted, and so did Corey Ford, Ed Zern, Lee Wulff, Harold Blaisdell, and Frank Woolner, and because they invited me to hunt with them, and because they were men of my father's generation who treated me like a man when I was a boy, and because they were writers who knew how to tell a story, and because they inspired me to try it for myself.

I hunt because Art Currier, Keith Wegener, Jason Terry, Rick Boyer, Skip Rood, Tony Brown, and Marty Connolly hunt, and because these are generous and intelligent men who don't take themselves too seriously, and who are saner than most. They love and respect the out-of-doors and Nature's creatures, and their friendship has made me a better man than I otherwise would be.

I hunt because the ghosts of beloved companions such as Bucky, Duke, Julie, Megan, Freebie, and Waldo prance through the woods, snuffling and tail-wagging, making game and pointing, and especially Burt, my beloved Brittany, who all loved to hunt more than to eat, and whose enthusiasm and indomitable spirit will forever inspire me, and because hunting dogs make the most tolerant friends. They are smarter in many ways than we are, and they can teach us things we otherwise wouldn't understand if we'd just pay attention.

I hunt because I believe Thoreau was right: "Fishermen, hunters, woodchoppers, and others, spending their lives in the fields and woods, in a peculiar sense a part of Nature themselves, are often in a more favorable mood for observing her, in the intervals of their pursuits, than philosophers or poets even, who approach her with expectation."

I hunt because I'm convinced, as many anthropologists argue, that prehistoric man was a hunter before he became a farmer, and because this genetic gift remains too powerful in me to resist. I do not need to hunt in order to eat, but I need to hunt to be fully who I am.

I hunt because it teaches me what it taught our earliest ancestors: the benefits of cooperation, inventiveness, division of labor, sharing, and interdependence. These are skills that bird hunters must master. Without these derivatives of hunting, our race would still be primitive. As the psychologist Erich Fromm observed, "[Humans] have been genetically programmed through hunting behavior: cooperation and sharing. Cooperation between members of the same band was a practical necessity for most hunting societies; so was the sharing of food. Since meat is perishable in most climates except that of the Arctic, it could not be preserved. Luck in hunting was not equally divided among all hunters; hence the practical outcome was that those who had luck today would share their food with those who would be lucky tomorrow. Assuming hunting behavior led to genetic changes, the conclusion would be that modern man has an innate impulse for cooperation and sharing, rather than for killing and cruelty."

I hunt because if I didn't, I would have seen fewer eagles and ospreys, minks and beavers, foxes and bears, antelope and moose, and although I do not hunt these creatures, I do love to enter into their world and spy on them.

I hunt because I love old 20-gauge double-barrel shotguns, and scuffed leather boots with rawhide laces, and canvas vests with a few old breast feathers in their game pockets.

I hunt for the scents of Hoppe's gun oil, camp coffee, wet bird dog, and frost-softened, boot-crushed wild apples.

I hunt for the whistle of a woodcock's wings and the sudden explosion of a ruffed grouse's flush, for the tinkle of a dog's bell and the sudden, pulse-quickening silence when he locks on point, for my partner's cry of "Mark!" when he kicks up a bird, for the distant drumming of a grouse, like a balky engine starting up, for the high predatory cry of a red-tail hawk, for the quiet gurgle of a deep-woods trout stream, for the soft soughing of the breeze in the pines, for the snoring of my companions, human and canine, in a one-room cabin, and for the soothing patter of an autumn rainstorm on a tin roof.

I hunt because it is never boring or disappointing to be out-of-doors with a purpose, even when no game is seen, and because taking a walk in the woods without a purpose makes everything that happens feel random, accidental, and unearned.

I hunt for the keyed-up conversation, for the laying of plans and the devising of strategies, for the way memory and experience spark imagination and expectation as we drive into the low-angled sunshine on an autumn morning, for the coffee we sip from a dented old Thermos, and for the way the dogs whine and pace on the way to the day's first cover.

And I hunt for the satisfying exhaustion after a long day in the woods, for the new stories that every hour of hunting gives us, and for the soft snarfling, dream-whimpering, and twitching of sleeping dogs on the back seat as we drive home through the darkness.

I hunt because it reminds me that in Nature there is a food chain where everything eats and is, in its turn, eaten, where birth, survival, and reproduction give full meaning to life, where death is ever-present, and where the only uncertainty is the time and manner of that death. Hunting reminds me that I am integrated into that cycle, not separate from it or above it.

I hunt with a gun, and sometimes I kill. But, as the philosopher Jose Ortega y Gasset has written, "To the sportsman the death of the game is not what interests him; that is not his purpose. What interests him is everything that he had to do to achieve that death—that is, the hunt. Therefore what was before only a means to an end is now an end in itself. Death is essential because without it there is no authentic hunting: the killing of the animal is the natural end of the hunt and that goal of hunting itself, not of the hunter. The hunter seeks this death because it is no less than the sign of reality for the whole hunting process ... one does not hunt in order to kill; on the contrary, one kills in order to have hunted."

I hunt to prevent myself from forgetting that everything I eat once lived, and that it is important to accept responsibility for living at the expense of another life, and that killing is half of the equation of living.

I hunt because it is hard, demanding, and sometimes dangerous work, and because performing difficult work well gives me pleasure.

And I hunt because it is fun, an intense kind of artistic game, and I like to challenge myself to do it well. As Aldo Leopold wrote: "We seek contacts with nature because we derive pleasure from them . . . The duck hunter in his blind and the operatic singer on the stage, despite the disparity of their accoutrements, are doing the same thing. Each is reviving, in play, a drama formerly inherent in daily life. Both are, in the last analysis, esthetic exercises."

I hunt because, in the words, again, of Ortega y Gasset, it gives me "a vacation from the human condition," which, all by itself, is a full and satisfactory reason.

Upland
Autumn

Chapter 1

PLAYING GUNS

I grew up in a little New England village surrounded by fields and pastures, woods and swamps, ponds and brooks. In those days half a century ago, before television and Little League and way before computers and virtual-reality games, we boys had to invent our own fun.

We spent our days wandering through the fields and woods and wading in the brooks and ponds, seeing whatever there was to be seen. We caught butterflies, frogs, and crayfish; we fished for horned pout, yellow perch, and eels; we collected rocks, arrowheads, and petrified wood; we learned the names of insects, wildflowers, and birds;

and we spent whole days poking around in the outdoors. Sometimes we just lay on our backs smoking the cigarettes we'd filched from our parents and looking up through the trees, and we made up stories about the shapes we saw in the clouds.

Nowadays such aimless and unstructured behavior is called "wasting time." When kids waste time, it worries adults and inspires them to organize clubs and teams and to raise money for uniforms in order to channel the kids' energies into more constructive and less worrisome activities.

When we neighborhood boys got together after school, we liked to play guns, a variation on hide-and-seek in which the winner shot the loser with his cap pistol, water gun, or index finger. It was a game of scattering through the woods, of hiding, stalking, and ambushing, of seeing without being seen. We skulked through the underbrush, hiding under bushes and hunkering behind boulders and tree trunks, trying to get a fair bead on some other kid before he spotted us. Then we aimed our make-believe guns and yelled, "Bang! Gotcha."

Playing guns, of course, was a hunting game—a game, I'm certain, that young boys played eons ago when their fathers took up their clubs and spears and left the cave for the real hunt.

Playing guns came naturally to us. Hiding, stalking, and ambushing required no instruction. No grownups showed us how to do it, organized it for us, helped us practice, taught us the rules, refereed for us, coached our teams, or argued on our behalf.

On the other hand, they didn't tell us not to do it, either. They didn't need to. We never confused our index fingers with real guns. Our fathers all owned real guns and taught us how to shoot them. Back then, we boys knew the difference.

We'd all been instructed about gun control. The phrase was familiar to us. It meant knowing whether a weapon was loaded and where the muzzle was pointing at all times and being sure the safety was on. Gun control meant aiming only at what you intended to shoot. It meant unloading your gun before you crawled under a barbed-wire fence, handed it to somebody else, or put it into the back seat of the car.

We didn't play with real guns. None of us ever did. We played with toys. Real guns were not toys.

Playing guns taught me how to move while appearing motionless. I could creep through the summer woods without cracking a twig or crunching a leaf. I could spot another boy by an anomalous shape, shadow, color, or motion. When I slithered on my belly from tree to tree, I was both hunter and hunted, predator and prey, and I knew, even if I couldn't articulate it, that I had tapped into something atavistic, natural, and important.

In those days, nobody saw anything dangerous or disturbing about a bunch of boys slinking through the woods trying to shoot each other with make-believe guns. Our fathers had done the same thing when they were kids.

When we outgrew playing guns, around the time we turned 10 or 11, many of my friends went on to other things that didn't involve guns, real or toy. But some of us, including me, hadn't lost our passion for slinking through the woods. Now we carried our Daisy air rifles and cardboard tubes of BBs, and we hunted dragonflies, grasshoppers, and moths. We also stalked toadstools, wildflowers, and leaves. Plinking, as it was called, was an honorable year-round sport for a country boy with a BB gun in those days. You don't hear much about plinking anymore.

When I became addicted to the bow and arrow, plinking evolved into stump hunting (which, I subsequently learned, was such a time-honored way for archers to practice hunting that it had a name: "roving"). The woods were full of targets for a kid with an imagination and a quiver full of homemade arrows. A clump of grass could be a rabbit; a rotten stump was a sitting grouse.

I hunted wild creatures, too. On a summer's evening, I crept along the edges of my local mud-bottomed, weedy ponds, hunting bullfrogs, which, I quickly discovered, were as alert for predators as one of my pals—or real fur—and feather-bearing game. I learned to spot the frogs by the two little humps their eyes made as they barely peeked up beside a lily pad. A sudden movement, a flickering shadow, a ripple on the water, or a flash of reflected sunlight, and those eyes would disappear. A careful stalk and a pinpoint shot—I aimed just behind those bulbous eyes—impaled the big amphibian to the mud bottom.

The first time I brought a bullfrog triumphantly home, my father said, "Must've been a good shot. Now you've got to clean it."

He didn't have to tell me why. I knew hunters ate what they shot. So I skinned the two meaty hind legs and put them in the freezer, and when I'd shot a few more bullfrogs, I fried their legs in butter.

I never did acquire a taste for frogs' legs. They tasted more like mud than chicken. But I liked hunting them, and so I kept eating them.

During the legal hunting season, I stalked live game with my bow—mostly gray squirrels, which abounded in the woods out back, but also rabbits, pheasants, and grouse whenever I might find them. I refused to try a shot unless I'd crept to within 20 feet of anything, a range that I knew would give me a good chance to make a killing shot and minimize the chance of losing a precious arrow. It had to be on the ground with no brush to deflect my shot, and I wouldn't try a shot at a moving target. I never did launch an arrow at a grouse or a pheasant, and even with all my playing-guns training, I spent a couple of seasons bow hunting for rabbits and squirrels almost every day after school in the fall before I finally shot one.

That fact that I didn't shoot anything—and rarely even shot *at* anything—didn't feel like failure. I crept close to plenty of squirrels. They were wily creatures, especially when they were on the ground where they knew they were vulnerable. I learned to recognize the sounds they made when scratching among the dry oak leaves for acorns, and usually I stalked them by ear before I got close enough to spot them. The trick was to move only when the squirrel ducked its head, to avoid making any sound on the crispy leaves, and to be absolutely motionless whenever my quarry lifted his head. I measured the success of my hunting by how close I could approach a squirrel before he scampered up a tree, not by the number I killed.

I shot only one squirrel with my bow, and that was the day I quit hunting them. I believe that, just once, every 12-year-old kid should gut-shoot a gray squirrel and hear its agonized, panicky squeal and see it try to crawl under a blowdown with an arrow sticking out of it. It's an unforgettable reminder that a squirrel is not a stump or a clump of grass or even a bullfrog, and that sometimes hunting isn't what you read about in magazines.

Since the day I shot a squirrel with an arrow, I have hunted only game birds with a shotgun.

The pastoral little truck- and dairy-farming town where I spent my childhood is now a densely populated suburb of Boston, but back when I was a kid I could load my double-barrel .410 in my backyard and spend a whole October afternoon hunting grouse and pheasants in the woods behind my house. Whenever the lady next door saw me heading out back with a shotgun under my arm, she'd call, "Good luck, Bill."

No farmer ever refused a kid with a gun permission to hunt on his land, nor would a local cop stop a boy who was riding his bike with a .410 braced across his handlebars and a handful of shells in his pockets.

Inevitably, the old farmers in my hometown sold out to the developers and moved to Florida. Local ordinances outlaw hunting or the discharge of firearms there now, and skulking through the woods is looked upon as unhealthy and unnatural. A boy who likes to play guns visits the child psychologist weekly.

Most of the kids I used to play guns with became adults who don't hunt wild game. They've gone on to different kinds of hunting. They are litigators; insurance salesmen; hedge-fund brokers; and headhunters who stalk, ambush, and bring down other prey, and they don't seem to understand that it's the same thing.

Many of them say they have happy childhood memories of slinking through the woods playing guns, but some of them have become holier-than-thou anti-hunting crusaders. I want to say this to them: No matter how hard you try, and whether you like it or not, you can't escape the fact that you're still a hunter, and before you criticize us, you should think about how you sublimate your own hunting instincts.

I still play guns. Now I use a shotgun instead of my index finger, and I hunt birds instead of other boys. But still, when I creep through the woods, moving without appearing to move, listening and looking for something anomalous, that primitive feeling returns, as strong as ever. It absolutely convinces me that I am still a wild creature, that the urge to hide and seek, to hunt and be hunted, lives in my genes—and yours—as it has since we first slithered out of the primal slime.

Chapter 2

THESE ARE OUR
GOOD OLD DAYS

When I was a kid, a day of grouse and woodcock hunting with my father began at the crack of dawn with a long drive from our house in the Boston suburbs into northern and western parts of New England. Such days inevitably ended with a long drive back home in the dark.

As the years passed, strip malls, highway cloverleafs, housing developments, and golf courses replaced our treasured alder thickets, poplar hillsides, and gone-wild apple orchards, and the commute to bird-hunting country grew increasingly longer. So did the distance between productive covers.

Finally just a couple of years ago I fled the suburbs and moved north and west to a little farm in a pretty New Hampshire village. This town is webbed with dirt roads and second-growth forest and abandoned farmland. There are very few No TRESPASSING signs. Everybody fishes and hunts.

My new hometown has a post office, a cash market, a library, and an inn that's sheltered wayfarers since 1789. There's a sheep farm, an apple orchard, and a couple of cornfields, and that's about it for commerce.

Our town dump recycles conscientiously, but it's officially called The Dump. It's that kind of a town.

My neighbors own fly rods, shotguns, and canoes. They raise goats, pigs, and chickens. They park backhoes, tractors, and pickup trucks in their barns. They read books, debate foreign policy, and drive long distances for good theater, first-run movies, and Yorkshire pudding, too, and they send their kids to college.

It's that kind of town.

In my new town, stone walls line every roadside. Old cellarholes are scattered through the woods. From my windows I can watch whitetail deer, wild turkeys, ruffed grouse, red foxes, black bears, and packs of coyotes hunt and browse in my fields. Barred owls and sharpshin hawks sometimes come swooping down to chase the chickadees and chipmunks from my bird feeders.

It's that kind of town.

In my town, there are twice as many miles of dirt roads as paved ones. It's mostly forest, meadow, mountain, and swamp. Rocky streams bubble through every crease in the hillsides. Pristine ponds nestle in every depression.

You could spend a lifetime tramping all those woods, driving all those back roads, and casting flies upon all that water. Unfortunately for me, I don't have a whole lifetime. But I'm giving it my best shot.

Aside from figuring out where the local trout lived, when I moved here, my number-one aim was to put together a string of local bird covers. For once in my life, I wanted to be able to spend the hunting season in the woods, not in the car. Whenever the spirit moved me, I wanted to be able to step outside, sniff the air, give my dog a whistle, and go bird hunting for an hour or two.

When you move to an unfamiliar part of the world and you've got a middle-aged bird dog—and when you yourself are looking back over your shoulder at the time when they started calling you middle-aged—scouting up a brand-new string of grouse and woodcock covers becomes a matter of some urgency.

With birds scarce and scattered to start with, and with the depressingly steady loss of even marginal habitat, lining up a day's worth of birdy places to hunt requires time and perseverance, not to mention a four-wheel-drive vehicle and a set of topographic maps—all of which are useless if you don't know what you're looking for.

Nowadays, before you can go hunting for birds, you've got to go hunting for covers that look like they'll hold birds.

It was all so different in the good old days.

I grew up hunting grouse and woodcock with my father and his friends. Burton L. Spiller, Frank Woolner, Corey Ford, Ed Zern, Lee Wulff, and Gorham Cross were some of Dad's friends. They were old-timers when I was a youngster.

When they talked about the good old days, "old days" meant the early decades of the 20th century when they were young men. By "good," they meant the bird-shooting.

In those days in New England, they told me, you could stuff a meatloaf sandwich into your game pocket, promise your wife you'd be back before dark with dinner, walk out the back door, slide a couple of shells into the old 12-gauge double, whistle up your setter, and set forth on a day of grouse shooting.

You'd put the morning sun on your back and wander more-or-less westerly. You'd criss-cross abandoned pastures studded with clumps of juniper and thornapple. You'd work the edges of old apple and pear orchards grown thick with briar and grapevine. You'd follow boggy streambeds trampled by cows and rimmed with alder, cut through woodlots half-grown to pine and birch, climb over oak ridges, prowl south-facing hillsides where the birch and popple still clung to their yellow leaves . . . and all along the way, they said, even with a mediocre dog you'd find plenty of birds.

New England in the first half of the 20th century was not far removed from the agricultural New England that, in the middle of the 19th century, had been 80 percent cultivated. In those days, many of the Yankee settlers had pretty much given up trying to farm that stingy soil, but the countryside had not yet been suburbanized and super-highwayed and Wal-Marted. Back then it was a network of small villages and scattered dairy farms laced together with dirt cartpaths. Otherwise, it was mostly overgrown pastures, field edges, wild orchards, tumbledown stone walls, and empty farmhouses with caved-in roofs and family plots gone over to milkweed and goldenrod.

Rural New England in the early 20th century, in other words, had become ideal grouse habitat, and when Burt Spiller and Corey Ford wrote their stories about it, they established the standard by which classic grouse hunting was measured.

A bird hunter didn't worry about scouting for covers in those days. The whole countryside was one big grouse cover. You just walked westerly for half the day, flushing birds here and there, shooting a few of them and missing plenty, which was okay because there would always be more. Around noon you'd stop beside a brook, empty your game pocket onto the ground, build a hot little fire, and boil a pot of water for your tea. You'd eat your meatloaf sandwich and munch the wild Bartlett pear or Baldwin apple you'd plucked from one of those old orchards.

Your setter would lie down in the brook to drink, then flop onto his side in a patch of sunlight for a snooze. You would lean back against a boulder and sip your tea and fire up your pipe and savor the memories and daydreams. And if the day was warm, you might take a little snooze yourself. After a while you'd speak to the dog, who would scramble to his feet, and you'd put the afternoon sun on your back and hunt your way homeward.

The days of the continuous grouse hunt didn't last, of course. It was just a moment in history, a blip in time between two eras. Dirt cartpaths got paved, farms became neighborhoods, villages became suburbs, grouse covers became golf courses, and No Hunting signs popped up like mushrooms after an April shower. Pastures, hayfields, and woodlots grew to mature forest, and ruffed grouse and woodcock sought out the increasingly isolated and scattered corners and pockets of cover that gave them the habitat they needed to survive. Burt and Corey and the others were cheerful men. They didn't wax nostalgic or talk wistfully about the good old days. They loved to go hunting. That never changed. But for the old-timers, grouse hunting in the middle of the 20th century, when I hunted with them, *had* changed. Now it meant driving the back roads and scouting hard for little patches of cover that looked birdy.

Those old-time grouse hunters knew, without having to analyze it, what they were looking for. Decades of prowling the autumn countryside and finding birds in some location—and not finding them in others—had imprinted patterns on their memories that defined the characteristics of good grouse cover. They instinctively understood that grouse needed tangly corners for protection from predators, sunny hillsides for warmth and feather dusting, open edges for quick escapes, apple, grape, and thornapple clumps for fancy dining, pine thickets for roosting, and rocky brooks for drinking.

When hunters found a place that looked right, they ran the dog through it to see if it actually held birds. If it did, they treasured it, gave it a name, and marked it on their topographic maps, and whenever they hunted there, they pulled their car far enough off the road so that other hunters, who would understand its significance, would not spot it.

I learned a lot by tagging along.

In my new hometown that first summer I discovered miles of dirt roads winding through woods, meadows, and old farmland, and I spent an hour or so almost every August afternoon driving them. I looked for breaks in stone walls, rutted cartpaths that petered out in the woods, fields without houses, old orchards gone wild, second-growth woodlots, brooks, pine thickets, sunny hillsides, and edges of any kind.

Nothing, I discovered, looks very birdy in August, when the woods are hot and thick with green foliage. It takes a lot of imagination to visualize how things might look in October.

In the evenings I scoured my topo maps, interpreted the symbols, recalled where I'd driven that day, and drew optimistic circles around possibilities.

My barber, my vet, my realtor's brother-in-law, and my neighbor at the end of the street were all bird hunters. Unlike the suburbs, in this town it seemed as if everybody owned a couple of setters and hunted birds. We talked about dogs and shotguns and compared versions of the good old days. I knew better than to ask their advice about places to hunt, and as friendly as they otherwise were, they never offered any.

Most of them, in fact, said they generally hunted, oh, a couple hours north of here.

So by the time Opening Day came around, in spite of my research and explorations, I hadn't identified a single grouse or woodcock cover where I felt confident I would find birds. I had only those hopeful circles on my maps.

I figured, okay, this season would be for reconnoitering. I'd hunt for covers, not birds. I'd check out all those marks on the maps, and I'd drive the roads and see how things looked in October. My goal for the season would be to line up a string of productive covers.

It turned out to be a summery autumn. The leaves clung stubbornly to the trees long after they should have fallen. The woods were dry and the air was warm, and it didn't feel much like hunting season. I found a few places that looked pretty birdy, and here and there my dog bumped—and occasionally pointed—the odd grouse or woodcock.

But I didn't find enough birds in any one place to mark it with a star on my map and give it a name, and I'd begun to think that I'd settled in this village too late, that the local boys were right, and that no matter where I lived, the good bird hunting would always be a 2-hour drive to the north.

A little after breakfast on the third Wednesday in October, Tony Brown knocked on my back door.

"Come on," he said. "Let's go for a drive."

"What's up?"

"Thought I might show you my grouse and woodcock covers."

I looked at him. "You kidding?"

He shrugged. "I don't get out much anymore. Bum knee. Don't want the good spots to go to waste."

I wasn't sure I believed him. I'd never noticed any limp. But I didn't turn him down.

Tony and I had run into each other several times around town. He'd commented on the Ruffed Grouse Society and Trout Unlimited stickers on my car. I'd fussed over the setter named Lilly who always rode in his back seat. We'd talked about going hunting or fishing sometime, but we hadn't gotten around to it.

On this Wednesday in October, Tony drove a lot of the back roads that I'd driven in the summer. He'd lived his whole life in this town. In his good old days, he said, he'd hunted hard and often, just walking through the woods all day.

Now and then he'd slow down and point. "You can't see it," he'd say, "but behind that stand of pines there's an alder run and a birch hillside. You can drive through that barway and tuck the car out of sight behind those hemlocks." And: "Doesn't look like much, but follow that old roadway about a half a mile and it opens to a grown-up field and an old orchard." And: "See that little stream? It comes bubbling out of a hidden swamp. Flight woodcock." There were ten or a dozen other patches of cover that had happy histories for Tony. Not a one of them lay more than 20 minutes from my back door.

I could have lived in the town for decades and never found half of them.

When we got back to my house, we spread my topographic map on the kitchen table, and Tony drew circles around the places he's showed me.

I explored some of Tony's covers that weekend. Two of them were empty, but looked good enough to try again. All the others held at least a grouse or two, or a scattering of woodcock, or both.

One of Tony's spots was at the dead end of a nondescript dirt road. My Brittany pointed a grouse while I was still loading my shotgun. There was a field bordered by a screen of pines (where we flushed a pair of grouse out of range), an apple orchard in one corner (another grouse there, shot at and missed), a hillside grown to head-high poplar (four woodcock, all pointed, two killed) that sloped down to a meandering, alder-lined brook (three woodcock, all survivors), a few acres of old slashing gone to second growth (three grouse, one pointed and killed), another field, a screen of pines . . .

It's a classic, really. Right out of a Burton L. Spiller or a Corey Ford grouse yarn or an Aiden Lassell Ripley watercolor. Tony swears nobody but the two of us knows about it. It takes an entire morning to hunt it right, and it's just a 10-minute drive from my house.

Maybe these will turn out to be the good old days after all.

Chapter 3

BURT AT 10

If, like me, you've grown leery of dog stories because they always seem to end with the death of the beloved old bird dog, let me assure you that Burt is lying on the floor beside me right now, pretending to snooze but ever alert to the possibility that I might push back my desk chair and say, "Wanna go hunting?"

He's the best dog I've ever owned. He was a puppy prodigy, and if I'd done my job better, there's no telling how excellent he could've been. But he's still awfully good. He's got some seasons left in him, and so do I. This isn't one of those death stories, I promise.

He was the pick of the males in the litter of Brittanies, a gift from my wife, just 8 weeks old when we fetched him from the breeder, a little orange-and-white pup with floppy ears and stubby little legs. When we let him out of the car, he pointed a moth.

I named him after my old gunning partner, Burton L. Spiller, who is known to literate shotgunners as "the poet laureate of ruffed grouse." "Burton L. Spiller's Firelight" is my dog's kennel name. I called him Burt.

I was working at home that summer, an ideal situation for training and bonding with a puppy. A hundred acres of woodland sloped away from the back of our house, and Burt and I explored every square foot of it. It seemed that he only needed to hear a command once to understand it, and he loved nothing better than to please the man who took him into the woods and fed him and allowed him to sleep on the rug beside the bed.

He was housebroken in a few weeks. He came when I spoke his name. He followed me from room to room. Everywhere I went, I took him with me. When I said "sit," "whoa," "come," or "heel," he did what he was told. "Get-in-the-car" was one of his favorite commands.

I read some books on dog training. Sorting out the contradictions and conflicting philosophies, I concluded that dogs instinctively want to please their masters, that messages should never be mixed, and that without the right genes, no amount of training would produce a good bird dog.

I didn't know if the corollary would also prove valid. I hoped that my well-meaning but decidedly amateur training program would not negate Burt's stellar genes. Both of his parents were grouse-trial champions.

The first time I teased him with a pheasant wing on a string, he locked on point. I let the wing lie on the ground. He didn't budge. I stroked his back and praised him, picked him up and set him down, and he just kept pointing that pheasant wing.

Burt was less than 5 months old, not even half grown, when October arrived. The books all agreed that he was at least a year shy of being mature enough to actually hunt, but I'd made it my policy to bring him everywhere with me, and even if all he did was run around in the woods while I hunted with my partners and their dogs, I didn't see how that could do any harm.

Besides, Keith Wegener's pointer, Freebie, would make a splendid role model for Burt, and so would Skip Rood's Brittany, Waldo. Both Freebie and Waldo were old dogs—hunting their last season, as it turned out. Both had developed into superior grouse and woodcock dogs. They'd slowed down and gone deaf in their old age, and neither of them could hunt more than a few covers before running out of steam. But they still had sharp noses, and both of them would rather point than eat.

Burt and I drove to Maine to hunt with Keith on Opening Day. The woods were tinder-dry, temperatures were in the 80s, and the leaves had not begun to drop. Freebie chugged through a couple of our best woodcock and grouse covers. They were empty. Burt had himself a nice morning of trotting around on his little legs and snuffling the air. It might have been my imagination, but he seemed to be watching Freebie out of the corners of his eyes.

We quit at noon, and as Keith said, "Burt did as good as Freebie."

The following weekend we hunted with Skip and Waldo. Our first cover skirted the edge of a pond. Burt and I followed the hillside, while Skip and Waldo took the string of alders that rimmed the pond.

We'd been hunting barely 5 minutes when I heard the quick explosion of a flushing grouse between us. I never saw the bird, but Skip, 100 feet off to my right, fired. A moment later he said, "Oh, hell."

"Miss him?" I called.

"No, damn it, I got him. Dropped him in the middle of the pond, and old Waldo sure as hell won't fetch him. I guess I'm gonna have to . . . wait a minute."

"What's going on?"

"Burt's swimming out there. I'll be damned. That bird is bigger than he is. He's got it in his mouth. He's swimming back with it. I don't believe this."

I hustled down to the edge of the pond, and I got there just in time to see half-grown Burt dog-paddling to shore with a full-grown grouse in his mouth. He brought it straight to me. I took it from him and thanked him. He kind of shrugged, shook himself dry, and looked at me, and it was pretty clear what he was saying: "Let's try that again."

Burt pointed his first woodcock that day. Actually he pointed his first six woodcock that day, and when I dropped one in some thick grass, he demonstrated his attitude toward retrieving woodcock. He flash-pointed it, crept up on it, then stood guard over it until I picked it up.

That afternoon, he and Waldo pointed at the same time. Waldo crept forward. So did Burt. From different angles they pointed again.

"They're roading a grouse," said Skip. "Waldo goes slow on grouse."

"Maybe that's what Waldo's doing," I said. "Burt doesn't know what he's doing."

"I think he does," said Skip.

The two dogs—the deaf old Brit and the half-grown pup—moved forward on tippy-toes, creeping, pointing, creeping again, converging from different directions. Finally they both locked onto a clump of juniper at the edge of a dirt road, about 100 yards from where they'd begun.

"Ready?" said Skip.

"I don't believe this," I said.

The grouse burst out and flew straight down the road, the easiest kind of straightaway shot.

I mounted my 20-gauge double and looked down the barrels. The grouse was flying directly at a house.

I lowered my gun. Skip had done the same.

"Would've been memorable to kill that bird," I said.

"Oh, I doubt we'll forget it," said Skip, "the way those two dogs worked."

Later that season I took Burt to a hunting preserve. We spent the day with a guide and one of the preserve's dogs, a lovely shorthair bitch who hunted planted pheasants and chukar every day. Burt had never sniffed a pheasant or a chukar.

The sleek shorthair and little half-grown Burt took turns pointing birds and honoring each other's points. I have no idea where he learned to do that.

That winter Burt grew up, and by spring he was long-legged and thick-chested, a dog, no longer a puppy.

In May, his breeder invited us to go for a run with one of his littermates to celebrate their birthdays. We met at a state wildlife management area and let the dogs out.

Zoom. They both disappeared. Now and then we caught a flash of white in the distance, one or the other of the two Brittanies crashing through the underbrush, running at full tilt, heading for the horizon.

I yelled. I screamed. I cursed.

They just kept running.

"I don't know what the hell got into him," I said. "He hunted beautifully last fall."

"He's doing great," said the breeder. "He's making wide sweeps, covering a lot of ground. He can really run. You should enter him in a field trial."

"I don't get it," I said, moaning. "He's acting like a crazy dog. He's forgotten everything he learned."

"In grouse trials," she said, "the dogs are supposed to run big. Burt looks like a winner, assuming he'd point if he found a bird. Would he?"

"Last fall he did. He loved to point. He pointed a damn moth the day I brought him home. Now, I have no idea what he'd do." I was thinking that my little prodigy had turned into a monster.

The breeder explained how Burt's superior grouse-trial genes gave him that terrific nose and those uncanny instincts, but they also gave him strong legs and boundless stamina and the burning desire to range as far as he had to—and as fast as he could get there—to find birds.

When he was 5 months old, she said, he had everything except the legs.

Now—and for the rest of his life—he'd have the legs, too, and I better get used to it.

We've had a lot of adjustments to make. Well, I have. I've struggled to convince Burt that he should hunt with me, that if he runs out of sight and beyond the sound of his bell he's not doing us any good. The classic grouse dog, I tell him, goes slow and hunts close, the way old Freebie and Waldo did, the way he himself did when he was 5 months old.

He doesn't buy it, and I remember that when Freebie and Waldo were in their prime, they liked to range pretty wide, too.

I've considered—and rejected—investing in a shock collar. I know that if I use it properly I might be able to convince him to hunt closer. But I can't bring myself to do it. It's not so much that I don't want to hurt him, although there is that. Mostly, I can't bring myself to punish him for doing what's been bred into him.

So I yell and scream and cuss, which doesn't seem to do him any harm and makes *me* feel better.

When flights of woodcock have settled into our covers, Burt works like my version of a classic upland bird dog. He hunts methodically, moving from point to point, looking over his shoulder now and then to make sure I'm with him, and if I want him to poke into some part I think he's missed, he doesn't seem to mind, although he makes it clear that if there were birds where

I wanted him to look, he would've found them without my help.

He still refuses to retrieve a woodcock. He'll find it, sometimes point it, and then he'll stand guard over it until I pick it up. If it's still alive, he'll gently hold it down with a paw.

The trouble is, in our New England grouse and woodcock covers, birds are scarce more often than not. Burt has no interest in barren cover, so he does what his genes tell him to do—he ranges wider and wider, searching for bird scent. He's the dog, he's got the nose, and his job is to find birds. I'm merely the man with the shotgun. My job is to shoot them.

Burt doesn't mind when I shoot and miss, but he hates it when, after all his work, I'm not in position to shoot.

I can't count the times when his bell has faded in the distance and I've been left standing there in the woods surrounded by silence. I listen. Not a sound.

So I do what any amateur dog handler would do. I yell.

Sometime later—a few minutes, maybe as much as 15 minutes later—I hear the bird flush in the distance, and pretty soon Burt comes trotting in.

We sit down and have a conversation.

I tell him I wish to hell he'd hunt closer. Pointing birds a quarter of a mile away from me, I explain, doesn't do us much good.

He tells me that I'm a slow learner and it's pretty discouraging. When will I start to trust him?

I ask him how he'd like to have one of those electronic beeper devices attached to his collar.

He says it would no doubt help me to find him when he's on point, but that infernal *beep-beep-beep* would be an abomination in a grouse cover, and on that subject, at least, we are in agreement.

Last May Burt turned 10. He's still in his prime. He can run like the wind and do it all day. He lives to find birds and point them for me.

I've come to understand that my job is to try to keep up with him.

Sometimes I dream of the day when Burt will slow down and hunt close, the way Freebie and Waldo did in their final seasons, when they were lame and deaf and on their last legs.

But that reminds me of stories where the dogs die in the end. I don't like those stories.

Chapter 4

SPILLER COUNTRY

Three or four times a year I take my old friend's shotgun from my gun cabinet, break it apart, check it for rust, and give it a good cleaning. It's a Parker 20, VH grade, a nice gun—beautiful, in fact—and perhaps modestly valuable. It looks like it's been hunted hard, and it has. Its bluing is worn shiny around the breech and at the ends of the barrels, there are dents in the stock, and the recoil pad is beginning to crumble. I've never bothered to have it appraised. It's not for sale, so why bother, although men who know its provenance have offered me what I'm sure is ten times what a shrewd gunsmith would pay.

I fit it together, snap it to my shoulder, trace the hard flight of a grouse cutting across the wall of my den, and remember all the birds it's shot—and all those I've missed with it. Then I sit back, lay the little Parker on my lap, close my eyes, and indulge myself in a moment of nostalgia—for the days when I tromped the uplands with Burt Spiller, and for the days when ruffed grouse prospered in Spiller country.

According to my father's meticulous journals, I hunted with Burton L. Spiller for the first time on November 10, 1951. Well, I didn't actually hunt in those days. I was 11, too young to carry a gun in the woods. Instead, I followed at my father's heels all day—through briar, alder, and mud, up hill and over stone wall and around blowdown. I didn't mind. Grouse hunting in those days was exciting enough even if you were just a spectator.

One English setter, two men, and one boy flushed 23 separate grouse that November day in Burt's string of southern New Hampshire covers. Burt, who was 65, walked the field edges and shot one of them with his sleek little Parker. My father dropped three.

Dad's journals suggest that was an average day back then.

In the 1955 season we became a regular threesome. At 9 every Saturday morning, Dad and I pulled up in front of Burt's white frame house in East Rochester. A leg o' mutton gun case, a black lunch pail, and a pair of well-oiled boots were already lined up on the porch, and when Dad tooted the horn, Burt came out, waved, and lugged his gear to the car. "Hi," he always grinned. "I've been expecting you. It looks like a wonderful day."

Burton L. Spiller was born on December 21, 1886, the right time; in Portland, Maine, the right place.

The 19th-century Maine farmers had opened the land. They moved rocks to clear pastureland and piled them along the edges to make Frost's "good fences." They planted apples—Baldwins, Gravensteins, Northern Spies, Russets, and Pippins. Second-growth birch, popple, alder, and hemlock pushed in when the farms were abandoned. Just about the time young Burt was old enough to carry a shotgun into the woods, classic grouse cover was everywhere. No wonder Burt Spiller became a partridge hunter.

He blasted his first grouse off the ground with his father's 10-gauge duck gun when he was 7. "Many, many times I have stood as I stood then," he wrote in 'His Majesty, the Grouse,' his first published story, "but there has never been another grouse or another thrill like that one. The kick is still there, as I presume it still is in the old 10-gauge, but—well—we are a little harder around the heart and shoulders than we were then."

A year later the Spillers moved down the seacoast to the little hamlet of Wells, and young Burt's lifelong love affair with the ruffed grouse was sealed. "Other boys of my acquaintance might content themselves with slaying elephants and lions and other inconsequential members of the animal kingdom," he wrote, "but I wanted none of that. Nothing but the lordly pa'tridge would satisfy me."

Eventually Burt bartered his bicycle and his watch for a 16-gauge double and "began to kill grouse regularly on the wing. I used the word 'regularly' advisedly," he wrote, "for the regularity was truly astounding. I shot a bird and killed it. Then I shot at 49 more and missed ingloriously. Then I killed another."

When he was a young man, he teamed up briefly with a pair of market hunters, an experience that steeped him in grouse lore and sharpened his wingshooting eye. Eventually he recognized "the difference between a sportsman and that reprehensible thing I was becoming . . . [so] I bought a bird dog and became a sportsman."

In 1911 Burton Spiller married and settled in East Rochester, New Hampshire, where he lived out the rest of his life. He was a blacksmith and a welder, and during the Great War he built submarines at the Portsmouth Naval Shipyard. He raised and bred prize-winning gladioli. He carved violins and made hunting knives. He hunted—not just grouse and woodcock, but ducks and deer, too—and he fished for brook trout and landlocked salmon.

Although he was pretty much self-educated, he began to write, working nights on his old Oliver typewriter. He sold "His Majesty, the Grouse" to *Field & Stream* in 1931. It was the first of 53 Spiller stories that magazine would print. The last was "Grouse Oddities," in 1967, when Burt was 81.

Between 1935 and 1938 the Derrydale Press published a Spiller book a year—all numbered, deluxe editions limited to 950 copies. First came the classic *Grouse Feathers*, then *Thoroughbred, Firelight,* and *More Grouse Feathers.* All have been reprinted one time or another. Those original Derrydales are treasures.

Around that time, someone dubbed Burt "the poet laureate of the ruffed grouse." The name stuck, as it should have.

In 1962, *Drummer in the Woods*, a collection of previously published grouse stories (mostly from *Field & Stream*), appeared. Burt also wrote a boy's adventure yarn called *Northland Castaways*, and in 1974, the year after he died, *Fishin' Around*, a collection of his low-key fishing stories, appeared.

I guess at one time or another, while the two of us were eating my mother's applesauce cake by a New Hampshire brook or bouncing over a dirt road between covers or trudging side-by-side down an overgrown tote road, Burt told me most of his stories. Whenever I reread a couple of them, as I do every time I take out the old Parker, I can hear Burt's soft voice, see the twinkle in his eye, and feel his finger poking my arm for emphasis.

In 1955, when I began hunting regularly with him, Burt was already 69 years old. He was a small, wiry, soft-spoken man, old enough to be my father's father. I called him "Mr. Spiller," as I'd been taught. But on the first morning of our first hunt he put his hand on my shoulder and said, "Burt, please. Call me Burt. When a grouse gets up, you can't go yelling 'Mark! Mr. Spiller' now, can you?"

I never heard him raise his voice, curse even mildly, or criticize or poke fun at any man or dog. He was a devout church-going family man who did not hunt on Sundays, even though it was legal in New Hampshire, or drink alcohol, but he was neither pious nor self-righteous.

A good joke, for Burt, was a joke on himself. His favorite stories were about the grouse that outsmarted him and the times he got lost in the woods.

He wore an old-fashioned hearing aid, the kind that plugged into his ear with wires running to the battery in his pocket. "I can hear pretty well," he told me cheerfully, "but sometimes I have trouble picking up the direction." It had to have been a terrible handicap for a grouse hunter, and it probably accounted for the fact that even in those years when partridge were bountiful in his covers, many a day passed when Burt never fired his gun.

When he saw a bird, though, his swing was as silky as I guessed it had been 50 years earlier. Once he and I were trudging up an old woods road on our way back to the car. Our guns dangled at our sides, and we were talking and admiring the way the October sunlight filtered through the golden foliage of the beeches that bordered the roadway and arched overhead. Dad and the dog were working their way along parallel with us somewhere far off to the left.

Suddenly Dad yelled, "Mark! Your way!"

A moment later a grouse crashed through the leaves and rocketed across the narrow road in front of us. It didn't make it. Burt's Parker spoke once, and the bird cartwheeled to the ground.

It was a spectacular shot.

Burt picked up the stone-dead partridge and stroked its neck feathers. Then he looked up at me. He shook his head and smiled apologetically. "Sorry," he said. "I should have let you take him."

He knew, of course, that the odds of my shooting that grouse were exactly the same as his own when he'd been my age: about 1 in 50. But that was Burt.

I was young and eager, and I tended to measure the success of a day's hunting by the heft of my game pocket. I learned how to hit flying grouse the old-fashioned way—by shooting often and relying on the law of averages—and as much as I missed, and as much as I expected to miss, I still tended to kick stumps and grumble and sulk when it kept happening.

Burt used to tell me, "Just keep shootin'. You can't hit anything if you don't shoot. And always remember: Every time you hit a flying grouse is a good shot."

I noticed that he never grumbled or sulked when he missed, although, to be accurate, he didn't seem to miss very often. Even on those days when birds were scarce, and it rained, and the dog behaved poorly, and nobody got any shots, Burt always had fun. Afterwards, when we dropped him off at his house, he always smiled and said the same thing: "A wonderful hunt. See you next week."

Gradually I learned to say the same thing at the end of every day—"A wonderful hunt"—and mean it. Burt taught me that.

He was moving a lot slower in 1964, and although he still wore the old hearing aid, he didn't seem to pick up sounds as well. Burt was 78 that year, but he still greeted us the same way when we picked him up in the morning: "Hi. I've been expecting you. It looks like a wonderful day."

On the second weekend of the season, after we laced on our boots at our Bullring cover for the day's first hunt, Burt said, "Uh, Bill? Can I heft your gun?"

I handed him my cheap Savage single-shot.

He threw it to his shoulder. "Comes up nice," he said. "Mind if I try it?"

"Sure," I said, though I couldn't understand why he'd want to.

"Here," he said. "You better take mine." He handed me his slick little Parker.

I carried Burt's gun through the Bullring, and he carried mine. I recall missing a couple of woodcock with it. Burt, straggling along the fringes of the cover, had no shots.

At our next stop, Burt picked up the Savage. "Never got to fire it back there," he said. "Mind if I try again?"

And so Burt lugged my gun around that day while I carried his Parker, and Dad's journal reports that I ended up shooting a woodcock, while Burt never dirtied the barrel of that Savage.

When we dropped him off, he said, "Why don't you hang onto that gun if you want to."

"Well, sure," I stammered. "I mean, I'd love to."

He smiled and waved. "A wonderful hunt, wasn't it?"

The next week when we stopped for Burt, it was my Savage that stood on his porch alongside his lunch pail and boots, and he carried it all day while I toted the Parker. Nothing was ever again said about it. We had swapped guns, and Burt had managed to accomplish it his own way, without ceremony. He never even gave me the chance to properly thank him.

I know for certain that Burton Spiller shot only one more grouse in his life, and it happened a couple of weeks after we'd exchanged guns. He was following a field edge while Dad and I were slogging through the thick stuff, and a bird flushed wild and headed in Burt's direction. Dad screamed, "Mark! Burt!" and I could hear the frustration in his voice, knowing that Burt probably couldn't hear him and wouldn't hear or see the bird.

But a moment later, from far off to our right, came a single shot.

We hooked over to the field and emerged behind Burt. He was trudging slowly up the slope, my gun over his right shoulder and a grouse hanging by its legs from his left hand.

Burt Spiller shot his last partridge with my gun.

The following Saturday—October 31, 1964—sometime in the morning, Burt fell. He never complained—didn't even tell us when it happened—but by the middle of the afternoon he had to call it quits.

He was still hurting the next week and the week after, and then the season was over.

Burt Spiller had hunted grouse for the last time.

During the next decade, Dad and I visited him periodically. He always had a smile and wanted to hear about the hunting. He continued to write stories and raise gladioli right up to his death on May 26, 1973.

A few months later, the old Savage came back to me with Burt's instruction: "For Bill's son."

Dad and I continued to hunt Spiller country for the next several seasons. Then one October we found a power line had cut the heart out of Schoolhouse. The next winter, Bullring became a highway cloverleaf and a Stop & Shop parking lot took the upper end of Tap's Corner. A couple of years later, the dirt road to The Old Hotel got paved over, and pastel-colored ranch houses sprouted up along both sides.

Burt's covers, those that remained, changed, too. Mankiller and Tripwire just didn't look birdy anymore. The hillsides that had once sprouted thick with juniper, birch whips, and head-high alders grew into mature pine-and-hardwood forests, and after a while we stopped hunting Spiller country altogether.

Besides, it would never be the same. It always seemed as if we'd forgotten the most important stop of all—at the white frame house in the village of East Rochester, where Burt would come to his door on a Saturday morning, grin and wave, lug his gear to the car, and say, "Hi. I've been expecting you. It looks like a wonderful day."

FIVE ACES

When I visited my father during the last autumn of his life, we liked to talk about how when he was feeling better we'd pile into my truck and spend a day or two driving the back roads to see if we could track down our old string of grouse covers. They were loaded with indelible memories that both of us cherished.

Somewhere along the line Dad had lost his priceless set of topographic maps where those old partridge hotspots were marked. We hadn't hunted them for close to 40 years, but we figured between the two of us, we'd recognize the old landmarks. We'd find them.

We'd run Burt, my Brittany, through the familiar old orchards, alder runs, field edges, and piney corners, just for old times' sake. Dad would walk along, and if we got a point, I'd hand him the gun and let him walk up the bird, the way he did with me when I was a kid and those old covers were busting with grouse.

My father was a crack wingshot in his day. I liked to imagine him dropping one last bird cleanly, and Burt hustling over, picking it up in his mouth, and bringing it to Dad's hand.

I guess we both knew it wasn't going to happen.

During those visits, I made it a point to urge my father to reminisce. He'd always been a pragmatic, stoical Yankee. He'd had a rich and fulfilling life, but a hard one, and he knew that the good old days hadn't always been so good. Nostalgia didn't come naturally to him.

But when it came to upland hunting, he admitted that those old days really had been awfully good.

"Remember Five Aces?" he'd say.

"A magical grouse cover," I'd say. "The best one ever."

"I'd like to see it again." He'd close his eyes and smile, remembering. Then he'd look at me and shrug. "No, actually, I guess I wouldn't. It won't be the same."

My father's New England encompassed the southern halves of Maine and New Hampshire. This, naturally, has been my New England, too. The countryside was different in the decade before World War II when he began hunting ruffed grouse. Winding roads, most of them dirt, connected dairy farms to villages. Otherwise it was mostly young second-growth forest, meadows, stone walls, and recently abandoned farmland—pastures, orchards, and woodlots growing thick with blackberry and thornapple, alder and poplar, pine and hemlock, oak and beech.

As Dad remembered it, it didn't much matter where you hunted. Grouse were scattered everywhere. A day of hunting meant wrapping a corned-beef-and-cheddar-cheese sandwich in waxed paper and stuffing it in your game pocket, cramming your pockets with 20-gauge shotgun shells, tucking your Winchester Model 21 under your arm, whistling up your setter, and setting forth. You'd put the morning sun on your back and head off, following the dog wherever his nose led him.

Around noon you'd stop, eat your sandwich, drink from a spring-fed brook-trout stream, and munch a wild Baldwin apple. If it was one of those warm October days, you'd lie back on the pine needles with the sun on your face, lace your fingers behind your neck, and snooze for an hour with your dog's chin on your thigh. Then you'd load up your shotgun again, put the afternoon sun behind you, and wander eastward until you got back to where you started from.

All along the way, Dad said, you'd find grouse—singles, pairs, sometimes whole broods. Even an average dog would point some of them, and even a mediocre wingshot would bag a few. My father always insisted that knocking down a flying grouse in thick brush was surely a triumph, but not really the main point of it. Grouse hunting was more about finding birds than shooting them. A good day was never measured by the heft of your game pocket.

By the time I started hunting with my father in the late 1950s, the New England landscape had changed, and grouse were harder to find. The meandering old dirt roads had been straightened, widened, and paved over, the abandoned farmland was being claimed by developers, and houses were popping up everywhere. Civilization was spreading over the countryside, and we couldn't just set off into the woods for a day's hunt. We did almost as much driving as we did walking. A day of grouse hunting meant six or eight stops at pockets of cover that we'd learned to depend on to hold a few birds. Dad called them "our string o' pearls."

A few of our covers sprawled over several square miles and occupied us for the better part of an afternoon. Most of them took little more than an hour to hunt. They were apple-and-pine corners, grape tangles, alder runs, poplar hillsides, and brushy edges bordering dense evergreens. They were usually good for a grouse or two, and when the woodcock flights were down, we'd sometimes find the ground whitewashed with their chalking.

Every season we lost a few of our old covers to housing developments, power lines, highway cloverleafs, and strip malls. Others just stopped producing. So we were always scouting for new covers. We scoured our topo maps for clues. We drove the back roads, always ready to take the one less traveled. Any break in a stonewall might signify an ancient cartpath that led to an abandoned farmyard or an old woodlot. We looked for apple orchards gone wild, alder-edged streambottoms, pastures grown to clumps of pine and thornapple, hillsides thick with second-growth poplar and birch—anything that looked birdy, which meant anything that reminded us of someplace where we'd found birds in the past. We didn't have much science for it. A birdy cover had a feel to it that was more than the sum of its parts.

Whenever a new spot produced some grouse, we circled its location on our map, gave it a name, and added it to our string o' pearls.

One day we were munching sandwiches and sipping coffee beside a little brook in New Hampshire. Duke, our old setter, snoozed on his side in a patch of October sunlight. Our open shotguns lay in the grass beside us. After a day and a half of hard hunting, all four barrels were still clean.

"Slim pickins," murmured Dad.

I nodded. "Mighty slim."

"First Chance, empty," he said. "Ditto Bullring. That one wild grouse in Mankiller. And what was it, two woodcock in all of Tripwire?"

"Maybe three," I said. "Duke bumped 'em. Never saw them."

"I dunno," he said. "Maybe our covers are just petering out. They don't look as birdy as they used to."

"They'd probably look birdier if we were finding birds in them."

Dad smiled. "Hand me that map, will you?"

He spread our topo map on the ground between us. Circles had been inked on it, marking the locations of our secret string of grouse covers. Mankiller, Clumps, Schoolhouse, Jackpot, County Line, Long Walk In, Tap's Pines, Bill's Folly, Traitorous Owl.

Dad squinted at the map, moved his forefinger over it, paused, then looked at me. "You up for an ex-plore?"

Brush scraped both sides of our station wagon as we crept over the old rutted roadway. It paralleled a rocky little stream that surely held native brook trout. The road, we happily observed, did not appear to have been driven on for a long time—perhaps, or so we wanted to believe, not since the farmer who cut it through the woods had loaded his family and his belongings into the back of his pickup and left for the last time decades earlier.

It ended at an abandoned farmyard on the edge of a sloping field grown to milkweed and goldenrod and sprinkled with gnarled Baldwin apple trees and clumps of juniper. The farmhouse on the hilltop was long gone. The roof and walls had caved into the cellarhole, but the field-stone chimney still stood, and an ancient lilac grew in the dooryard.

We got out to look it over. The field rolled down to a stand of poplars that gave way to a screen of evergreens. Off to the right, a hillside thick with brush, briar, and birch rose to a ridge lined with oaks, and behind the cel-larhole, the glimmer of a brook wended through a string of alders.

"Well," I said. "What do you think?"

"Looks kinda birdy," said Dad. "Worth a look-see."

By the time we got our shotguns loaded, Duke was pointing in the poplars that rimmed the bottom of the field. Dad shot that grouse. A minute later he dropped another one that rumbled out from a clump of hemlocks. He doubled on a pair of woodcock that helicoptered up from a patch of alders, and then he nailed another grouse that we surprised pecking apples in the corner of the old orchard. In between, half a dozen grouse and at least as many woodcock escaped. I shot at several of them.

When we got back to our car, Dad emptied his game pocket, picked up one of his grouse, and stroked its crest with his forefinger. "Eureka," he said softly.

It had been the best three hours of bird hunting that we could remember.

"Do you realize," I said, "that you just went five-for-five?"

He grinned. "Of course I do." He reached into the back seat, pulled out our map, drew a circle on it, then arched his eyebrows at me.

I took the pen and wrote "Five Aces" on the map.

Hippie House, Stick Farm, John's Knoll, Arnold's Picker, Red Bloomers, Lost Eyeglasses, Marilyn Monroe, The Old Hotel. Five Aces, especially. Just reciting their names floods me with half a century's worth of memories: Dad, of course. Burt Spiller, Gorham Cross, Frank Woolner, Harold Blaisdell, and Corey Ford, the men of my father's generation who shared their wisdom and their grouse covers with me. Keith, Art, Skip, Tony, Marty, and Jason, bird-hunting partners of my generation. Macko, Bing, Duke, Cider, Bucky, Waldo, Freebie, Burt, and Lilly, bird dogs both mediocre and gifted, all lovable. Points and retrieves, flights of woodcock and broods of grouse, shots made and shots missed.

I don't suppose my hunting partners and I will ever find another Five Aces, but we keep looking. We scour our topo maps, drive the back roads, track down rumors. Every year we do manage to come up with a few new grouse covers.

This past season we found a brood of grouse at the end of a rocky road that crosses over a river and cuts through some woods. We're calling it Grandma's House.

Curse Buster is the little pocket of apple and evergreen where Jason dropped his first grouse after nearly two seasons of shooting and missing.

And the old pasture where a grouse caught me—literally—with my pants down and my empty shotgun on the ground, and the only thing I could shoot at it were words as it glided brazenly across the open field, we've named Expletive Deleted.

The October after my father died, I piled Burt into my truck and we went hunting for Five Aces. When I finally found the narrow, rutted old dirt roadway, I saw that it had been paved, widened, and straightened and lined with mailboxes. The rocky stream that ran alongside it now flowed through culverts and concrete gutters. Half a dozen more-or-less-identical colonial-style houses had sprung up around a cul-de-sac in the field, and they'd bulldozed the hilltop flat where the old cellarhole had been. More houses were scattered along the new roads that had been cut through the woods.

I'm glad my father wasn't with me to see it.

Chapter 6

LITTLE RUSSET
FELLERS

Freebie's tail was a blur as she snuffled and snorted a slow zigzag through the alders. She stopped abruptly, poised with her weight canted precariously forward.

"We finally got a point over here," I called to Keith on my right flank.

The Stick Farm, our morning leg-stretcher, had been empty. John's Knoll, the sun-drenched slope where a mix of poplar, pine, and apple grew—also empty. Arnold's Pasture, muck-bottomed and alder-studded, fertilized and trampled by the old farmer's dairy cows—empty too. We had startled some spawn-minded native brookies from a rocky pool in the little rill that meandered behind the Hippie House. But no woodcock.

There didn't seem to be a woodcock in the entire state of Maine.

I'd been studying reports and talking with biologists, game wardens, and hunters for the previous several years. Everyone agreed that woodcock were in trouble.

I'd seen the evidence myself, but I'd fooled myself into discounting it. I'd blamed the dog. I figured we'd been looking in the wrong places or mistimed the flights. I didn't want to believe it. But on this day, the second Saturday of October, usually prime time, I finally believed it. The woods were empty of the lovely little game birds. Woodcock were definitely in trouble.

I eased myself forward. "Easy, Freeb," I murmured. "Good girl. Steady, now." She rolled her eyes back at me.

I stepped in front of her.

The round little bird rose with its characteristic twitter: slow motion, angling sharply upward to the top of the alders, pausing there as if it might lose its struggle against gravity, then slanting to its left, quartering away.

My shotgun had mounted itself, and the bird was a lollipop over the muzzle. An easy shot. A gimme.

"Bang," I said.

The woodcock continued to fly.

I fired my second verbal barrel: "Bang." Then I lowered my gun and watched it glide into the alder swamp beyond the field.

Keith came over. "Did I hear a woodcock get up?"

"Yep."

"About time. Freebie bust it?"

"Nope. She did good."

"You didn't shoot," said Keith.

"Safety stuck," I lied.

"I thought I heard you say something," he said. "Swearing at your gun again, huh?"

"I gotta do something about that damn safety," I said.

"Get a line on the bird?"

"Nope."

He shrugged. "No harm. One woodcock doesn't make much of a meal. Anyway, I kinda like knowing it's still out there."

"Me, too," I said.

According to the Seneca Indians, after the Maker finished creating all the creatures of the earth, he looked around and realized he had some leftover parts lying around. There was a small pile of feathers—not big flashy ones, for those had been taken by the glamorous species he had already created, but drab earth-toned shades of gray and brown. There was a head, but the brain was upside down, the ears were misplaced in front of the boggled eyes, and the beak was disproportionately long. The Maker found a chunky little body, stubby legs, and sturdy but graceless wings. It was an ill-matched assortment of parts, but because the Maker hated to waste anything, he put them all together and called it a woodcock.

The Maker realized he'd shortchanged the little bird in the body parts department, so he compensated by giving the woodcock an extra infusion of courage, stamina, wisdom, and mystery.

Ornithologists and others who speak Latin call the woodcock *Philohela minor*, which means "little sun lover."

It's actually a misnomer. Woodcock travel by night and hunker in dark, boggy places by day (although those of us who hunt them are never surprised by where we find them). Observers who saw them poking their long beaks into the ground in search of worms, their main nourishment, called them "bog suckers" and "mud snipe." They've been called "Labrador twisters" and "mud bats" because of their erratic flight, and "night partridges" because of their nocturnal ways.

Their most common nickname is "timberdoodle," which perfectly captures the personality of the little bird. "Doodle" derives from a German word meaning "fool" or "simpleton," hence "doodlebug." Woodcock, in fact, look like big insects, and they behave like pranksters. "Doodle" also means "divining rod," which conjures up the image of a small bird poking its long beak into the wet earth.

Frank Woolner suggested "whistledoodle," an apt nickname that recognizes the distinctive sound of a flushing woodcock. As far as I know, however, "whistledoodle" hasn't stuck.

My old friend Burton L. Spiller affectionately called them "little russet fellers." I always liked that.

Sometime around the middle of March, the little russet fellers return home to New England from their winter sojourns in places as far south as Louisiana. They've been flying northward for several weeks, for thousands of miles, impelled by—by what? By the changing angle of the sun? By the sniff of warming air? By a new moon phase? By the northward shift of prevailing winds? By Nature's most powerful urge of all, the instinct to procreate?

It's a combination of all of these things, no doubt, fine-tuned over countless generations and firmly embedded in woodcock DNA to assure the survival of their species.

One thing is certain: The family urge is upon them. They fly by night, rest by day, and feed hardly at all, beating relentlessly northward to the precise field or hillside where they were born. Their hormones fuel their single-minded purpose. The males stake out their territory, and the females wait nearby to be courted. It's called the "singing ground."

Biologists have yet to find a more reliable method for taking their annual American woodcock census than by counting the birds they hear singing in the evenings during their mating season and comparing the numbers with those of previous years.

The comparisons haven't been positive for a long time.

For me, spying on courting woodcock has always been a springtime ritual. As much as cutting pussy willows, watching the ice break up in my pond, spotting my first robin, seeing my first mayfly, or casting to my season's first trout, hearing my year's first woodcock song marks the certain end of a long New England winter.

The American woodcock is a peculiar, private, funny-looking, and altogether lovable little bird. Aside from a small breed of peculiar, private, funny-looking, and generally lovable sportsmen who hunt them with pointing dogs and double-barreled shotguns, few people are aware of the woodcock or would recognize one if they saw it.

Those of us who have made the woodcock's acquaintance find them elusive, mysterious, admirable, and altogether lovable. We worry about them, for their populations have been declining steadily for more than 40 years. Their habitat is disappearing steadily, it's as simple (and complicated) as that, and there is no reason to think they will recover. We still hunt them in the fall, because we know we are the least of their problems, and because hunting them teaches us to understand, admire, and love them.

Some of us might sometimes choose not to shoot them. But we still love to hunt them with good pointing dogs.

And we seek them out in March, when they return from their wintering grounds, so that we can celebrate the arrival of springtime with them.

I pick a cool March evening after a warm day, that delicious time of year when old snow still huddles in dirty patches under the evergreens but the fields lie brown and bare and the earth is soft and the brooks run full with snowmelt. I hunker at the edge of a winter-flattened meadow facing the pewter-and-pink western horizon, not far from my house in southwestern New Hampshire, and I watch the light fade from the sky. I know it will start about the time the evening's first star winks on.

No matter how expectant I am, the sudden buzz always startles me, both by its proximity and by its harshness. It sounds like the scrape of a thumbnail across the teeth of a metal comb. It is, technically, a song, but it's hardly melodious. It's called, inexplicably, a "peent."

The little bird struts self-importantly on the bare ground not 20 feet from where I crouch. His chest is inflated and his long beak jabs rhythmically at the ground. He swaggers and bobs back and forth like a wind-up toy, buzzing like a summertime cicada. In fact, a woodcock looks like a large, boggle-eyed insect.

Abruptly he flushes. With a musical whistle of wings, he angles across the field. Then he begins to spiral up into the pale evening sky. He rises higher and higher until he disappears from sight, although I can still hear his distant, muted twitter.

A moment later he reappears, zigzagging and parachuting back to earth like an autumn leaf on a soft breeze. As he descends, he utters a different tone, a liquid kissing note. He lands beside me, almost precisely at the spot where I first spotted him. He peents, preens, struts, then flushes again, full of heedless hot-blooded passion. He repeats his elaborate, intensely self-absorbed dance several times while the light fades from the sky and the night grows chilly.

Soon it is full dark. The performance has ended. I stand, gaze up for a moment at the star-filled evening sky, then walk back out of the woods. The air still feels winter-cold. But I am warmed by the certain knowledge that my woodcock have returned for one more season, at least, and spring has finally come to New England.

Chapter 7

CAMP TIMBERDOODLE

When Kenny called to fine-tune our plans before last October's Annual Camp Timberdoodle Partridge and Woodcock Extravaganza, he told me he was bringing along a friend, if that was okay by me. "He seems like a good kid," Kenny said. "Young guy name of Josh, just moved up from Delaware, of all places. Full of piss and vinegar. He's all excited. Passionate about bird hunting, the way we used to be."

"Speak for yourself," I said. "I'm still pretty passionate."

"Lately," Kenny said, "my passion seems to come more from remembering how it used to be in the good old days, rather than actually looking forward to it. Know what I mean?"

"Yeah, I guess," I said. "Memory, not anticipation. I think we dwell too damn much on the good old days."

"This kid, Josh," said Kenny, "he doesn't have any good old days to dwell on. No old days of any description, good or bad. No memories. Nothing but anticipation."

"Well," I said, "it'd be nice if we could give him some memories. Grouse and woodcock need more passionate young friends. The main question is, does he snore?"

"How the hell would I know?" said Kenny.

Camp Timberdoodle sits on the banks of Arnold's Pond up in the northwestern corner of New Hampshire where, on a road atlas, there are no roads. You won't find Arnold's Pond on your atlas, either. It's just a dammed-up section of a small trout stream that eventually joins a river that wanders south and east into Maine. Kenny's father, Arnold, built the dam to hold trout and attract waterfowl. You can still find the ruins of the old man's duck blind on the point of land near the foot of the pond.

Kenny's sister got Camp Timberdoodle when Arnold died, which Kenny says was the old man's perverted idea of a joke, and even though his sister lives in Seattle and hasn't been east since the funeral, never mind the fact that she doesn't hunt, she refuses to sell the place to Kenny. He says she's just like his old man. Loves to bust his balls.

Every year, Kenny has to ask her permission to use the place for our annual October weekend. Groveling, he calls it. Every year he expects her to turn him down, and then he ends up feeling unnaturally grateful to her when she says okay.

Kenny, Ike, and I have been going to Camp Timberdoodle for 20 years over whatever weekend in October falls closest to the 19th, the date that, according to Kenny, marks the peak of the woodcock migration in northern New Hampshire. Kenny's camp is in the middle of what we believe to be the best grouse and woodcock hunting left in all of New England, such as it is, which, of course, isn't anything like the good old days.

Camp Timberdoodle is your basic bird-hunting camp: woodstove, kerosene lamps, arm-powered water pump, two-holer out back. There's a small kitchen, a big living room, and one bedroom, where Kenny always sleeps. He claims he's earned that privilege because he's the one who has to grovel before his sister every year. The rest of us unroll sleeping bags on the living room floor with whatever dogs we've brought along and take turns yelling at each other to stop snoring.

Kenny, Ike, and Jenny, Ike's new setter pup, along with a young guy who looked disconcertingly like Brad Pitt—Josh, I assumed—were on the screen porch drinking coffee and watching some mergansers on Arnold's Pond when I got there. Kenny made a show of looking at his watch and said, "About time." Ike shook my hand without bothering to stand up. Jenny pushed herself to her feet and went over to Burt, my Brittany, so they could sniff each other's privates.

The young guy stood up and held out his hand. "I'm Josh," he said. "It's great to meet you."

"Me, too," I said. "Do you snore?"

He smiled uncertainly. "I don't think so."

I kept Burt at heel as the six of us—four men and two dogs—strolled down the long sloping meadow to the alder-rimmed brook. The hillside on the other side of the brook was awash in sepia and burnt umber, the colors of October in northern New Hampshire. Overhead, the midday sun burned thin and yellow through a layer of lacy clouds. There was a pleasant nip to the air; chilly, but not cold. It smelled of frost, mud, and dead milkweed.

We planned to split the brook. Kenny and Ike headed for the far side with young Jenny. Josh, Burt, and I would take this side.

While we waited for the others to cross the brook, Josh told me that he and his bride had recently moved up from Delaware, where he'd hunted stocked pheasants and wild ducks. Loved all kinds of bird hunting, he said. He carved decoys, devoured sporting books and magazines, read everything Burton L. Spiller had ever written. He'd met Kenny at a Ducks Unlimited meeting that summer.

He was, he said, "totally psyched" to hunt grouse and woodcock.

"Burt's pretty psyched himself," I said. "He's going to go charging right down to the corner of the stonewall down there. He knows there are two grouse there. Problem is, the day's first cover, he's all crazy and will probably bust 'em wild."

"Two grouse, huh?" said Josh. "Cool."

"At least two," I said. "It's way cool."

"I've never shot a grouse," he said.

"Hustle down to that corner," I said, "and be ready."

"Or a woodcock, either," he said. "Actually, I've never even shot *at* one."

"Today's your day."

I waited for Josh to get into shooting position down by the brook, though I figured it was futile. Burt was sitting beside me coiled like a steel spring, and I knew when I said, "Okay," he'd bolt. He always did in the day's first cover. He'd ram full speed into the thick stuff, and if there were birds, he'd either be out of sight when he pointed them, or he'd bust 'em wild and bark at them.

Unlike Kenny and me, who lived off our memories, Burt was fueled entirely by anticipation. He loved to hunt—hell, he *lived* to hunt—and I liked the fact that a middle-aged dog, unlike most of the middle-aged men I knew, could still be so charged up. I didn't really mind that he rammed around like a crazy person in our first cover, though if he happened to bump a grouse and give chase, I'd certainly yell at him, just to remind him of what was expected of him.

The thick stuff that bordered the brook featured head-high alders, muddy bottoms, field edges, blowdowns and briars, young birch and poplar, some old apple trees, and a scattering of hemlock, juniper, and thornapple. Mixed cover, and birdy as hell.

Part of me was thinking: *I hope there are no birds there. I don't want Josh to see Burt screw it up.* Another part of me retorted: *Don't be a fool. It's always better to find birds in good-looking cover than not find them.*

Burt sat there, quivering, whining, and rolling his eyes.

Josh, on the edge of the brook, appeared to be quivering, too. "So what do we do?" he said. "I've never done this before."

"You keep the brook in sight on your right," I said. "I'll be off to your left, and if he does it correctly, Burt will work the cover between us. Stay even with me. If you see a grouse, shoot it."

"How'll I know where you are?" he said. "It looks awful thick in there."

"You'll hear me. I'll be the one yelling at the dog. Ready?"

Josh grinned. "As ready as I'll ever be, I guess."

I tapped the top of Burt's head. "Okay," I whispered.

Zoom. Burt tore headlong into the brush, and in about a minute his bell was a distant tinkle that I could barely hear over the gurgle of the brook.

I yelled at him, of course; to no avail, of course.

Then I couldn't hear his bell at all. When that happens, it normally means he's on point, except in the day's first cover it probably means he's just galloped out of hearing range.

I yelled some more, then stopped to listen. No bell.

"Be ready," I called to Josh. "He might be pointing."

A minute later I heard Burt yipping way off in the distance. Okay. He had been pointing. Then he either busted the bird, or it flushed. Either way, he was chasing it. Marvelous.

As I stood there, I realized that Burt's yipping was getting louder. "Get ready," I called to Josh.

The grouse came on silent wings, skimming the tops of the alders, heading right for me. He passed over my head so close I could see his beady little eyes.

I turned and took him going away.

"Get him?" called Josh.

"Yep," I said, casual-like, as if I fully expected to hit any grouse I shot at.

About then Burt came crashing through the underbrush. When he saw me, he skidded to a stop and looked at me, and if dogs could talk, he would've been saying, "Oh, hello, there. Fancy meeting you here."

"Dead bird," I told him. "No thanks to you. Go fetch." I pointed at where I'd marked down the grouse.

Burt was back a minute later with the bird in his mouth.

I took it from him. "Thank you," I said. "It works better if you hunt closer to me, you know?"

He nodded, then went over to the brook, lay down in it, and started drinking.

Ten minutes later Burt locked on point near a tangle of blowdowns on the edge of an old clearcut. "We got a point," I called to Josh. "Hustle on over here."

I went up behind Burt. "Easy," I said. "Steady, now."

Burt rolled his eyes back at me.

Josh appeared. "Oh, wow," he said. "Look at that."

I gestured at an opening in the trees. "The bird'll fly that way. Swing around over there."

When I saw that Josh was in position, I eased around Burt, paused, then took two more steps.

The grouse burst out from under my feet and headed Josh's way. He raised his gun, pivoted, swung, hesitated . . . and then the bird was gone.

At that moment another grouse flushed and cut to the left. I dropped it with a longish crossing shot.

I kicked at the blowdown a couple times, but no more grouse came out.

By now Burt was retrieving my bird. He brought it to me, and I cradled it in my hand. Two shots, two grouse. This was unusual for me.

Josh came over. He was grinning. "Man, that was pretty. Like a painting or something, seeing Burt pointing, and those birds come crashing out, and you shooting it, and the dog fetching it. Awesome!"

I smiled and nodded. It *was* rather awesome.

It would have been more awesome, though, if Josh had dropped his bird. He wouldn't get an easier chance all weekend, and he didn't even get off a shot.

I was thinking: *This kid wasn't embarrassed, frustrated, angry, or apologetic at failing to pull the trigger on an easy going-away shot at a grouse. He didn't even curse or make excuses. It was kind of weird. Kenny or Ike—well, me too— would've been screaming.*

But it also occurred to me that we'd had at least one solid point, probably two, moved three grouse, taken two shots, and dropped two birds, all in about 20 minutes. A lot of seasons, that would constitute a decent full day of hunting. I wondered what Josh was thinking.

A little farther along the brook, three more grouse rumbled out unseen from a screen of hemlocks, and a few seconds later four shots echoed from the other side of the brook, and a minute after that, Kenny and Ike yelled, almost in unison, "Damn it! How in the hell?"

We kept going. Burt bumped a couple of singles, one of which flew past Josh, who said he never saw it. I shot a woodcock that Burt pointed along the brook, and 50 yards farther on I dropped the first and missed the second of a possible woodcock double, just to show Josh that it was okay to miss once in a while.

Meanwhile, Josh hadn't fired his shotgun, even though, in addition to those grouse, three or four woodcock had twittered up in front of Burt's points and headed his way.

After a couple hours, Kenny, Ike, and Jenny crossed the brook, and we stopped to compare notes and reconnoiter. They'd killed a grouse and three woodcock. Jenny had pointed one of the woodcock—her first ever.

So far, the new dog was doing better than the new hunter.

"These birds all fly so fast and crooked," said Josh. "There's always a tree or something in the way. I can't get on them. Every time I think I'm on one, it goes sideways or just disappears."

"There's your problem right there," Kenny said. "You're not supposed to think. You just gotta shoot. You want to kill grouse and woodcock, you've got to shoot fast and think slow."

"Like Kenny," Ike said. "Kenny's a notoriously slow thinker."

Josh smiled tentatively. I figured he was trying to decide when, if ever, he should take us seriously.

By the time we got back to our starting point at the brook, I estimated that we'd flushed about a dozen grouse and close to twenty woodcock. Kenny, Ike, and I stopped shooting at woodcock after we each bagged a brace, our personal daily limits. Along the way, we killed two more grouse.

We missed plenty of times, too, which gave us the opportunity to curse the birds, the dogs, the trees, the sun, the Red Gods, plus each other. Many years in the woods together had taught us to curse imaginatively, eloquently, and fulsomely. We believe that creative cursing is a time-honored and essential element of upland bird hunting.

Josh, I noticed, watched us with a kind of shy amusement.

As we headed back to our trucks with our shotguns broken and the dogs at heel, Kenny leaned close to me and said, "So how's the kid doing?"

"He seems to be having fun," I said.

"That was an awfully good hunt," he said. "We haven't moved that many birds in a long time."

I nodded. "He never fired his gun. He keeps waiting for a wide-open shot, I guess."

"Big change from ducks over the water and pheasants over a field."

"Yeah," I said. "But the thing that worries me is, he just keeps smiling. I mean, doesn't he know how to swear?"

Back at Camp Timberdoodle, we lit the lamps and got a fire going in the stove, and I made a vat of Bill's Famous Chili. We washed it down with some beer that Josh had brought. Kenny, Ike, and I took turns telling stories about the Good Old Days of New England bird hunting. Josh sat on the floor with Jenny's chin on his leg and didn't have much to say.

When Ike and I woke up the next morning in the living room, Josh was gone. We found him in his sleeping bag out on the porch. "You guys snore pretty loud," he said.

We didn't find as many birds on the second day, but we found enough to make it a good hunt. Jenny pointed her first-ever grouse. Ike kicked it up and missed with both barrels, then fired off an admirable string of expletives, all of which hit the mark dead on.

Josh managed to touch off a few shots at woodcock. He didn't hit anything, but he seemed pleased with his progress, although he did pass up several opportunities for heartfelt swearing.

Finally, on our third and last day, he knocked down a straightaway woodcock over one of Burt's points.

Burt doesn't retrieve woodcock. He finds them and stands over them until I come to pick them up. If it's wing-tipped, he puts a paw on it.

I cradled Josh's woodcock in my hand, smoothed its feathers with my forefinger, then handed it to him. "Congratulations. Your first woodcock."

Josh smiled. "Lucky shot. About time."

"They're all lucky shots," I said.

We quit in the middle of the afternoon. We had to go back and muck out Camp Timberdoodle before the long drive home.

At our trucks, we put away our shotguns and took off our shooting vests and sat on the tailgates sipping coffee.

"Damn good trip," said Ike. "A helluva lot better than last year."

"Sorry I didn't shoot better," said Josh.

"Yeah," said Kenny, "we never miss."

Josh smiled. "I had no idea what to expect," he said. "I've read everything I could get my hands on about grouse hunting in New England, but this was . . . it was awesome."

"It's not always like this," said Kenny.

"Truthfully," Ike said, "we haven't had hunting like this for years."

Josh shrugged, and it was hard to tell if he believed us.

"Where are the dogs?" Kenny asked.

Burt was over at the edge of an alder thicket, pointing. Little Jenny was stretched out behind him, honoring his point.

"Lookit that," murmured Ike. "Lookit my bird dog."

"Go shoot those birds," I told Josh.

He smiled, loaded up, and headed over to the dogs.

"I feel bad for him," said Kenny as we watched Josh move up behind the dogs. "Poor kid's got no perspective. We've found a helluva lot of birds this weekend. Anything that doesn't measure up to this, he'll be disappointed."

"At least we've given him something to remember," I said. "Now he's got a couple of good old days all his own."

As we three old-timers watched, Josh eased up beside the dogs, paused to say something to them, then moved ahead. Two woodcock helicoptered to the tops of the alders, and Josh's gun came up. He fired twice. The birds kept going.

"Dammit," Josh said conversationally, and he muttered a few other things I couldn't quite make out.

"Hear that?" Ike said. "The lad's catching on. I do believe we'll make a bird hunter out of him yet."

Chapter 8

HOW TO MISS
FLYING GROUSE

Sporting magazines periodically publish articles titled, with minor variations, "How to Improve Your Grouse-Shooting Odds." It's earnest, practical stuff, often accompanied by charts that factor such variables as wingspeed, angle of ascent, shot size, muzzle velocity, choke, and pattern, along with inspiring diagrams depicting ruffed grouse and clouds of birdshot colliding in midair.

Actually, I'd be tempted to take it all as mean-spirited satire. If you hunt grouse, you know what I mean.

These articles prey mostly on the false hopes of frustrated beginners. The so-called expert writers take gleeful delight in pointing out that while grouse don't fly as fast as sea ducks, doves, or many other shotgun targets, they rarely fly straight or at constant speeds, and they are uncanny in their ability to put trees and brush between themselves and a man with a shotgun. Like crafty old major-league pitchers, grouse love to throw change-ups, curveballs, sinkers, and knuckleballs. They dart, dip, and move at unpredictable angles. Then, just often enough to keep you off balance, they throw a high hard one at you. They usually flush from unexpected places at unexpected times. Then there are factors such as sun (which is always in your eyes), hilly and brushy terrain, uncertain footing, wind, and—well, if it isn't one thing, it's another.

Still, claim the writers, you will shoot more birds if you follow their ten (or seven or twelve) surefire tips.

According to the expert authors (I'm summarizing here), readiness and sharp reflexes help. You have to be mighty quick and alert to mount your gun, take aim, get your muzzle out there in front of the bird, and snap off a shot—in 1 second. During that time a ruffed grouse can fly nearly 60 feet. Even a woodcock moving at a leisurely 25 mph—under a head of steam, woodcock can fly quite a bit faster—travels 37 feet in that single second.

These sober and informative (or tongue-in-cheek, it's hard to tell) magazine essays generally advise aspiring upland marksmen to put in a lot of time at the sporting-clays range, invest fortunes on customized shotguns, and practice dry-mounting and swinging in the privacy of their own living rooms. Twice a day, 15 minutes per indoor practice session, is about right.

It makes pretty entertaining reading, if you've got a taste for masochism. But it occurs to me that these articles might dupe naive readers into believing that shooting a flying grouse is actually a skill, implying that it can be learned and perfected.

Anyone who's hunted with shotguns for a while knows that this is arrant nonsense. I've been tromping the uplands for nearly half a century now. I've hunted with skeet and sporting-clays pros, grizzled outdoor writers, and old-time market hunters, as well as rank beginners. I've kept a detailed journal of my days afield, and I can assure you that the only useful wisdom on the subject of hitting flying grouse with a shotgun resides in the Eternal and Immutable Law of Averages.

Wingshooting skill has nothing to do with it.

Here are the hard facts: For every twelve grouse flushed, four escape unseen; of the eight that the hunter glimpses, four are out of range, disappear too quickly, or otherwise evade getting shot at; of the four shots that the hunter takes, three are misses.

To be more specific: For every twelve grouse my partners and I have encountered in 45 years of upland hunting, we've shot exactly one. I've seen the hunting logs of other upland gunners, including some who write how-to-shoot-grouse articles, and their records are virtually identical to mine.

Oh, I know, we all have a hot streak now and then, and hunting with one of those precious hotshot grouse dogs can temporarily up the odds—just as those long cold streaks when you can't do anything right drops them. I'm talking about the long haul here.

Still, with all due respect for those writers and other experts who recommend shooting quick or shooting slow; snap shooting or leading and following through; understanding angles, flight speed, and wind direction;

practicing and calculating or relying on instinct; using bigger or smaller shot sizes, lighter or heavier shotguns, doubles or autoloaders, big or small bores, tight or open chokes; or consulting hypnotists and psychics . . . the truth is: IT DOESN'T MATTER.

Over the long haul, you'll shoot one out of every twelve grouse you encounter, and there's nothing you can do to change it.

All those how-to-shoot-grouse articles, therefore, serve no purpose except to cruelly raise the expectations of unwary readers and to amuse the rest of us. If you expect to learn anything, prepare to be disappointed, because no matter what combination of skill, luck, practice, perseverance, woodsmanship, and experience you take afield, you will fail to connect eleven out of twelve times. No magazine article can change that.

The Law of Averages will take care of that happy one- in- twelve triumph for you. Hitting grouse isn't the problem One memorable success, eleven failures. That's it.

The real question is: How are we supposed to handle those eleven other times?

What grouse hunters *really* need is a repertoire of explanations, excuses, and alibis to account for a 92-percent rate of failure.

Here's where my half-century of missing flying grouse can help. So, as a service to grouse hunters old and young, I have scoured my journals and consulted my partners and other expert grouse-missers, and I have compiled a compendium of excuses which, I am confident, any grouse hunter can adapt to his needs.

Nothing beats sharp reflexes, a nimble imagination, and decades of practice. The master of the alibi can snap off a quick excuse in a wingbeat. Some gifted gunners seem to be blessed with a God-given talent for excuse making. They just pick it up from the beginning. They're naturals. They are to be envied.

For the average hunter, though, nothing beats a lot of practice. Novices shouldn't expect to come up with anything truly original or inspired right away. Begin with modest expectations. Don't be ashamed to plagiarize. Remember: Most good excuses have already been used. Because they're good, they have survived the test of time. They still do the job. Even experienced alibiers fall into predictable patterns. You can learn from the experts.

The rules of effective alibi-making are few and simple:

1. Be prepared. You know with absolute certainty that eleven out of twelve grouse will elude you. Going into a partridge covert without a handy supply of excuses is like going out to sea without a life jacket. You're inviting disaster.

2. Keep in mind that there is an explanation for every miss. Your job is to come up with it without hesitating or bumbling. "I thought I was right on him," or, "Geez, I missed again," or, "Dunno what happened that time," are not excuses.

3. Never blame your own lack of skill. "I didn't lead him enough," or "I lifted my head just as I shot" mark you as an amateur of the alibi. Remember: It's not your fault. Instead, deflect the blame to your equipment. "I had him centered. This old gun never did pattern no. 8s well." Or, "The old blunderbuss just hasn't hung right since I lost all that weight." In a pinch, haul out the

oldest and most shopworn excuse of all: "My safety stuck again." It still works.

4. Emphasize the difficulty of the shot you missed. "He was out of range. Never should've pulled the trigger." Or, "Just caught a glimpse of him as he darted around that tree. It would've been a miraculous shot."

5. Never give the bird any credit as that's just a backward way of blaming yourself. "He caught me off guard" or "He kept that big pine tree between us" simply makes you appear inept. Instead, shift the blame to the elements: "That big pine jumped right in front of me, took the whole load. I was right on that bird, too. Come here. Take a look at this tree." Or, "The sun popped out from behind the clouds just as I squeezed off my shot. Blinded me for a second." Or, "I swung right up against a poplar sapling." Or, "I was horse-collared by a grapevine. Did damn well just to get a shot off." Your gunning partner (who, remember, wants you to accept *his* excuses with a straight face) will nod and murmur sympathetically.

6. Whenever possible, deflect blame onto your partner. Be cautious—you must be subtle and phrase these alibis carefully lest you provoke a did-not/did-too discussion that will convert all future excuses into debates. Try these: "I could've taken him easy, but he was headed your way. I pulled off at the last second so you could take him. What happened?" Or, "You kinda got out in front a little back there, didn't you? If we'd done it right, we'd've had that bird cornered." The advantage of this tactic, of course, is that it immediately challenges your partner to come up with a better excuse than you did, and you have preempted the

entire blame-your-partner category of alibis. When you accept his excuse—as you must—you've assured yourself of an understanding audience for all the rest of yours, however weak they may be.

7. Blame the dog. If it's your dog, it's easy. After you miss, simply yell, "Burt! Damnit! What do you think you're *doing*?" To guarantee sympathy and understanding, mumble something about Burt's ancestors, that charlatan trainer in Vermont, your wife (who insists that Burt sleep in the bedroom), or your kids (who throw objects for Burt but fail to use the command "fetch"). If it's your partner's dog, it's trickier, but still possible. Never blame his dog directly. Instead, shift the burden of alibi-making to your partner. "Was Mack over there with you when that bird got up?" Or, "It looked like Mack was making game, and the next thing I knew . . . "

8. That one-in-twelve occasion, when your shot brings a puff of feathers and a dead bird, if you handle it deftly, sets you up for the rest of the season. Never credit either your skill or your luck. Instead, use your moment of triumph to establish the excuses you know you'll be needing. "I thought I was right on him, but the sun was in my eyes. I just kept swinging and shot at the blur." Or, "My safety kept jamming. Got that shot off in the nick of time." Or, "I think Freebie bumped him. That bird was nearly out of range when I shot."

In the beginning, it's advisable to hunt alone. Practice your alibi-making on an imaginary partner. At first you'll fumble around and your excuses will sound pretty lame.

But if you work at it, you'll find that acceptable alibis begin to tumble swiftly and gracefully from your lips.

When you start believing them yourself, you're ready to hunt with a partner.

If you spend enough time in the woods, eventually a grouse will give you an unbelievably easy shot—say, a slow right-to-left across an open field. You will, of course, miss it. Nothing in your well-practiced repertoire of alibis has prepared you for this. You'll be tempted to shrug and blurt: "How could I have missed? Never had a better chance in my life."

Don't do it. Instead, recognize that this is the moment of truth, the ultimate challenge, the occasion that years of practice have pointed to.

Now is the time to convert disaster into triumph. Look your partner in the eye, shake your head, and say: "Did you see how slow and straight that grouse was flying? It was too easy. No challenge. It was all I could do to restrain myself from shooting him."

Your partner will be awed. And isn't that what grouse hunting is all about?

Chapter 9

THE WORLD ACCORDING TO GRAMPA GROUSE

If any word here recalls to old or young some nostalgic remembrance of warm October sun, crisp leaves, incredible shots, frosty mornings, the tangy scent of old apples, the feel of cold gun barrels, a loved dog or elusive birds, I shall be repaid and please remember: Any allusions or references to persons or places are purely malicious.

—Partridge Shortenin, Grampa Grouse, 1949

The first time I hunted grouse with Keith Wegener, a bird flushed from the edge of a swamp while I was clawing through the limbs of a fallen tree. I screamed "Mark!" as I tried to disentangle myself from a wild grape vine and scramble into position to get a shot. Just as I fired at the flash of gray tailfeathers, my foot caught on a half-buried strand of barbed wire and I fell flat on my face.

I was combing the twigs out of my hair and checking my gun barrels for dents when Keith wandered over. "Well?" he said. "Bring down any feathers?"

"No, damnit," I answered. "The blowdown had me horsecollared and a tripwire snagged me, and besides, that jeesly pat turned out to be a sidewinder. I think I'm gonna grudge him."

Keith frowned at me. "Huh?" he said. "Do you speak English?"

"Sorry," I said. "I forgot you aren't a member of the Grouse Shortener's Association."

Once in a pre-dawn kitchen when the grouse shorteners were assembling their gear for a weekend in New Hampshire, the young son of Gorham Cross's partner stumbled downstairs. When the boy's father introduced him to Mr. Cross, the tot rubbed the sleep from his eyes, hitched up his pajamas, and politely held out his little hand as he'd been taught to do. "Good luck, Mr. Grouse," he mumbled.

Gorham Cross became Mr. Grouse after that, and he was delighted to become Grampa Grouse when his first grandchild was born.

He was my father's regular grouse-hunting partner when I might have been that sleepy-eyed boy—and even before—in the 1930s and '40s, and he died just about the time I was old enough to carry a shotgun in the woods. So I became Grampa Grouse's successor. I know Dad was happy to have his son for a partner. Still, my father missed Grampa Grouse to the day he died.

As much as my partners and I have loved grouse hunting, I'm convinced that no one ever had more fun at it than Grampa. Even half a century later, Dad still chuckled and shook his head at Grampa Grouse's sayings, foibles, superstitions, and off-kilter wisdom. Sometimes I'd catch him staring off into space with a soft smile playing on his lips, and I knew he was remembering those days he shared with Grampa when New England was dotted with tumbledown cellar holes and intersected with stone walls, when every dirt road led to an abandoned farmyard, when the alders and birch whips grew head-high and the old pastures were studded with juniper clumps and thornapple, when the field edges were thick and brushy, and when ruffed grouse pecked frost-softened Baldwin apples in every overgrown orchard in New England.

My father's October and November weekends were devoted to bird hunting in those days. Grampa, clad in his grouse-hunting costume, would pull his old Jeep into our driveway before sunup on Saturday morning. In his Monday-through-Friday life, Gorham Cross was a respected and well-to-do Boston businessman. But in the woods he wore faded and briar-tattered jeans, a work shirt gone to holes at the elbows, and a shapeless felt hat. In a cold autumn kitchen with a bird-hunting weekend ahead of him, Grampa was as jittery and jangly as the dogs, who skittered their toenails on the linoleum and whined at the back door when they spotted the guncases and hunting boots piled in the kitchen. They couldn't wait to get going. Neither could Grampa Grouse.

And then the Jeep would appear again after dark on Sunday evening, and Grampa and Dad would unload their birds—always, at least in my memory, a lot of birds.

Grampa Grouse had a round, ruddy, laughing face and a crown of white hair, and I remember my father's affection for his older friend—and his grief the day Grampa died. He was just 59, way too young.

Dad's old hunting log records the fact that I began tagging along on some of his weekend hunts with Grampa Grouse in my 11th autumn. I was too young to carry a gun in the woods, so I dogged my father's footsteps through the thick stuff, and I began to learn what a flushing grouse sounded like and where the birds lurked and how quickly a man had to shoot to hit one.

On the long rides up and back to their New Hampshire grouse country, and on the shorter rides between covers, I sat in the back seat with the dogs. I leaned forward and folded my arms across the top of the front seat so I could listen to the men. They talked grouse talk. Their language was peculiar, decorated with words and phrases that made no sense to me at first.

Luckily for those of us who knew him, Grampa Grouse wrote a book. He called it *Partridge Shortenin*—"being," as Grampa expanded his title, "an instructive and irreverent sketch commentary on the psychology, foibles, and footwork of partridge hunters." In 1949 he published it privately in a limited edition of 100 copies, dedicated it to his wife, "the self-styled Shotgun Widow," and gave copies to his friends. Its pages are unnumbered, reflecting, as Grampa noted, "the fragmentary and haphazard manner in which these yarns have been written and printed."

Grampa presented a copy of his book to the young son of his hunting partner, and I still have it. It is, I have been told, treasured among collectors. I have been offered a lot of money for my tattered copy.

For those of us who reread *Partridge Shortenin* every couple of years, it's a journey back to days of innocence and wonderment that we otherwise might forget. They were my childhood days—and Grampa's, too, because his enthusiasm for upland hunting was childlike right to the end.

Grampa theorized about grouse cycles, but never did he acknowledge the possibility—now, half a century later, in fact—that beloved covers such as Timbertop, Limberlost, Rocky Hill, Binney Hill, Crankcase, Tap's Pines, and Clayte Brown's Picker would one day be cut down and paved over, or would just evolve into mature forests; nor did he ever consider that the day would ever come when broods of partridges would no longer burst from the corners and fly their grooves.

Oh, how Grampa loved grouse, and the men and dogs who hunted them! Every day was an adventure for Grampa, and every hunt was a war. Grouse were canny adversaries, worthy enemies, and outsmarting them demanded Machiavellian strategies—that failed as often as not, to Grampa's consternation . . . and delight.

And woe to the fox or hawk who dared to poach on Grampa's beloved grouse. He always carried two loads of high-base Remington 00 buckshot—"varmint shells"—in his shooting vest in case he encountered a grouse predator in the woods.

As much as he loved partridge, though, Grampa loved his hunting partners above all else. "Companionship is the essence of bird shooting," he wrote. "When you get a pal whom you can hunt with, eat and sleep with, drive and endure with for two or three long days, you have a real shooting partner."

If I'd had Grampa's book for those back-seat hours, perhaps I'd have been able to follow the men's front-seat conversations more easily. And today, if I were to lend it (which I won't), I wouldn't have to translate myself to my hunting partners.

So here instead, for the uninitiated, is a primer of the grouse-hunting language, as spoken by Grampa Grouse and my father and the other members of the Grouse Shorteners' Association:

batteries (n.)—energy (of hunters and dogs); "Let's sit a spell and recharge our batteries."

battery acid (n.)—what you pour into a steel Stanley Thermos; coffee.

been-through (adj.)—previously hunted, usually by rabbit hunters; "Not a single biddie in the whole cover," mourned the Old Master. "Looks like it's been-through." Grampa Grouse believed that the explanation for all empty covers was that they'd been-through by rabbit hunters. He refused to acknowledge the possibility that his secret covers could be known to other grouse hunters who might've been-through them, or, even worse, that no birds lived in them.

biddie (n.)—ruffed grouse (see: pat).

birdy (adj.)—tense and alert, with wagging tail and snuffling nose (describing the behavior of a bird dog); also, likely to hold grouse (describing the appearance of a cover); "Spotting birdy cover is a matter of observation and experience."

blowdown (n.)—fallen trees and limbs (see: hellhole, mankiller, picker, horsecollar).

boiler (n.)—bladder; ("bust a boiler"—urinate); "All you dogs can bust your boilers," the driver announced.

bogged down (adj.)—lethargic; a breakfast of pancakes and sausages can leave a hunter bogged down all morning.

chalking (n.)—the distinctive white splashes left on the ground by woodcock, a sign that woodcock are present or, more likely, that they have recently departed.

chassis (n.)—body (referring either to a dog or a person); "Old Dog, shame!" quoth I. "Your chassis is dirty!"

disagreeable (adj.)—agreeable; "I'm disagreeable to most anything," chimed the Professor.

doodle (n.)—woodcock; short for "timberdoodle."

guess-what (n.)—the ingredients in sandwiches prepared for hunters by shotgun widows; "a guess-what sandwich."

groove (adj.)—predictable; "There's groove birds that fly the same jumps every day till you get them."

grudge (v.)—to curse; "Grudging is equivalent to putting a ju-ju on a bird. It is a challenge and duly respected by all."

hellhole (n.)—thick cover (see: picker, mankiller).

horsecollar (n.)—a tangle, usually a combination of blowdown, briars, and grapevines in a hellhole, mankiller, or picker, that ensnares a hunter and prevents him from snapping off an accurate shot; "We always found ourselves on the wrong side of a tree or horsecollared in bull-briers when a bird got up."

iron rations (n.)—Hershey chocolate bar.

jeesly (adj.)—all-purpose malediction, typically applied to imaginary rabbit hunters who have been-through a grouse cover.

mankiller (n.)—a hellhole or picker where a hunter is sure to get horsecollared.

Mark! (exclam.)—what grouse shorteners scream to alert their partners when a grouse flushes; for those who have been yelling "Mark!" all their lives, it becomes a conditioned reflex; even when hunting alone or just tromping through the woods without a gun, the explosive flush of a grouse causes long-time partridge shorteners to scream "Mark!" the way a dog drools at the sight of his food bowl.

pants-draggers (n.)—the flotsam and jetsam that hunters carry in their pants pockets; Grampa never entered the woods without ten shotgun shells for birds and two for varmints, a "dollar" pocket watch, iron rations, dog candies, a compass, a Boy Scout knife, a cloth bag for license and money, a waterproof container of matches, tissues in a waxed-paper sandwich bag, and a pencil flashlight.

parlor (n.)—the prime part of a woodcock cover; a place where woodcock gather to eat worms and exchange gossip about the foibles of partridge and woodcock shorteners.

pat (n.)—ruffed grouse; short for "pa'tridge."

picker (n.)—thick cover (see: hellhole and mankiller)

pickins (n.)—abundance; e.g., "slim pickins" or "easy pickins."

popple (n.)—a species of deciduous tree; poplar.

ravine (n.)—narrow valley or gulch; rhymes with "grape vine" and pronounced with the accent on the first syllable (RA-vine).

road bird (n.)—grouse that is spotted in the road; "Road birds are exasperatingly tempting. They are harder to harvest, by legitimate methods, than a bird started in cover but are always worth a try, for they may traitorously lead the hunter to other birds or to a new cover."

seed bird (n.)—a grouse that hunters don't shoot and that will therefore live to reproduce; excuse for missing an easy shot; "I pulled off him at the last minute. Figured we should leave a seed bird."

sentinel bird (n.)—a sly grouse that lurks on the edge of a cover, often in a tree, whose job is to flush loudly at the approach of hunters, alerting all the other grouse in the cover.

shortenin' (v.)—shooting and killing; shorteners are those who shoot and kill grouse and thus reduce, or shorten, their numbers.

shotgun widow (n.)—wife of a grouse hunter, esp. in October and November.

sidewinder (n.)—a grouse that flies at a sharp angle to the side, usually up or down a steep slope; often grudged.

slot bird (n.)—a grouse whose escape route is a narrow opening in the cover.

stink bird (n.)—all species of birds except grouse or woodcock; stink birds mislead inexperienced or overly eager dogs into making game and pointing, to the embarrassment of their owners.

tripwire (n.)—any kind of fence wire, often barbed, left lying on or just above the ground for the specific purpose of causing grouse hunters to stumble.

twig (v.)—poke with a stick; "When twigged in the eye, ask for time out, or take it, and wait until it clears up."

VWF (abbrev.)—Veritable Winter Fairyland; the appearance of a grouse cover after a late-autumn snowstorm.

wall bird (n.)—a grouse perched on a stone wall alongside a dirt road; most wall birds are former road birds that moved at the approach of a vehicle.

WGC (abbrev.)—Wild Goose Chase; a fruitless hunt; more frequently used in reference to grouse than geese.

Nowadays, it seems, the southern Maine covers that Keith and I treasure—Hippie House, Stick Farm, and Rusty Bedspring—come up empty, or close to it, all too often.

We rarely spot road birds or wallbirds anymore, and few doodles seem to gather in their old favorite parlors.

But at least now, after rambling over dirt roads together for all these years, Keith and I can communicate. Last Saturday, for example, we were feeling pretty bogged down by noontime, so we sat on the ground and leaned our backs against an old stonewall to recharge our batteries. We'd had slim pickins that morning. We'd heard the flush of one sentinel bird, and Burt had bumped a pair of doodles out of their parlor on the sunny side of John's Knoll, and that was it.

"Well," observed Keith between bites of his guess-what sandwich and sips of battery acid, "another WGC. All them pickers must've been-through by a bunch of jeesly rabbit hunters."

Chapter 10

FRANK WOOLNER'S LOVE AFFAIR WITH RUFFED GROUSE

A mong shotgunners who have made their acquaintance, ruffed grouse consistently arouse the strongest passions. All agree that this partridge is the smartest, wildest, hardest-flying, and altogether most challenging, frustrating, and lovable game bird on two wings.

Such a bird deserves a passionate chronicler, and no man I've hunted with or whose stories I've read was more passionate—about life, writing, friends, hunting and fishing, the outdoors in general, and ruffed grouse in particular—than Frank Woolner.

Woolner's life overlapped those of Burton L. Spiller, William Harnden Foster, Gorham "Grampa Grouse" Cross, and John Alden Knight, who all wrote timeless elegies to the ruffed grouse. Anybody who has read Spiller's *Grouse Feathers* and *More Grouse Feathers,* Foster's *New England Grouse Shooting,* Cross's *Partridge Shortenin',* or Knight's *The Ruffed Grouse* will agree that Frank Woolner's *Grouse and Grouse Hunting,* published in 1970, deserves an honored place on the bird-hunter's shelf alongside those older classics.

"Mine is a love story," Woolner wrote, "a sometimes personal treatise on the game bird that is more important to me than wild geese coursing an autumn sky, than black ducks cupping their wings and dropping into the blocks, than woodcock spiraling over the alders in the red hush of an October twilight."

Like most outdoor writers of his generation, Frank Woolner was a generalist, a jack of all trades and a master of most of them. He spent his life in the New England out-of-doors, passionately devouring whatever the season offered. He hunted upland birds and waterfowl, rabbits and squirrels, foxes and deer. He cast flies and drifted worms for brook trout, and he heaved live eels and wooden plugs into the Cape Cod surf for striped bass. When no game or fish was in season, he tromped the fields and forests anyway, absorbing nature's stories.

I grew up believing that men like Frank Woolner had the best job in the world. He fished and hunted and called it research. He went out and had adventures, then he wrote about them—and people gave him money for it. What a life!

Woolner's prose came out of his typewriter so clean and pure that he fooled me into believing that writing was easy, a delusion that persisted until I tried doing it myself.

Back in the 1930s and '40s, my father edited a sporting magazine called *Hunting and Fishing*. He bought Frank Woolner's first outdoor story and thereby helped to launch a career that lasted half a century.

My father launched a lot of other careers, too, and being the man he was, he usually ended up hunting and fishing with the writers he did business with. I was the lucky kid who got to tag along. Thus I made the acquaintance of a whole generation of sporting writers, including Frank Woolner.

Frank shared the tangled grouse coverts near his home in Shrewsbury, Massachusetts, with me, and later, when I decided I wanted to emulate his enviable lifestyle, he shared his wisdom on the writing business with me, too, as he did unselfishly with countless other novice outdoor writers. He taught me that it wasn't as easy as it looked, and he encouraged me when I needed encouragement.

Frank learned to write the same way he learned to catch stripers and hunt grouse—by trying, erring, and pondering it, then trying some more.

I'm not sure how many stories Frank sold after that first one that my father bought. Several hundred, certainly. He also published half a dozen books, including *Grouse and Grouse Hunting* and *Timberdoodle!*, its companion piece on woodcock, which is also a classic.

He wrote about hunting and fishing, true, but he also wrote about the chill of an autumn afternoon and the warmth of the sun's rays when they reflect off a pewter sea. He wrote about robins, bats, wildflowers, stonewalls, mosquitoes, and tree frogs—which Frank called, delightfully and evocatively, "the bells of springtime."

When Frank Woolner died in 1994, he was still counseling young writers, turning out silky prose on all manner of outdoorsy subjects, and sharing his hard-earned wisdom on the comings and goings of striped bass, bluefish, flounder, and weakfish for *Salt Water Sportsman.*

And that, I've learned, is how outdoor writers do it. They hunt, they fish, they wander around in the woods, and then they write until they drop. They never retire from doing what's in their blood.

What a life!

Frank Woolner began writing in a simpler time, when the morality of the blood sports was rarely challenged by animal-rights activists or anti-gun crusaders. A thoughtful man, however, didn't need a challenge to think about it. "I make no apology for being a gunner and an angler," he wrote, "but I am a hunter without malice and maybe a fisher who seeks much more than any limit catch of trout."

Today's naturalists might raise an eyebrow at Frank's readiness to shoot grouse predators, but his reasoning was neither simplistic nor hard-headed. Nobody understood the complexities of nature's ways better than Frank Woolner. "It is characteristic of well-meaning yet ill-informed nature lovers to insist that all predators are beneficial," he wrote. "This product of wishful thinking contains just enough truth to make it dangerous."

On the other hand, he understood that "extremists who rant that every flesh-eating bird or mammal should be shot on sight betray an abject ignorance of wildlife dynamics."

Woolner's middle ground, whether you agree with it or not, is based on a commonsense understanding of nature's interconnectedness, coupled with his unabashed love for ruffed grouse. "If I am hunting in a state where the great horned owl is unprotected," he declared, "I will shoot each and every one that shows in upland cover . . . I have a bone to pick with do-gooders who have convinced legislatures that the great horned owl should be protected at all seasons. Ill-informed nature lovers are robbing Peter to pay Paul: the ruffed grouse suffers."

Grouse and Grouse Hunting, which has been reprinted several times since 1970, most recently in 1999 by The Lyons Press with the title, *Grouse Hunting Strategies*, contains equal parts of natural history and hunting lore. The book is proof that a respect for nature and a passion for hunting go hand-in-hand. As much as he loved grouse, I can vouch for the fact that Frank hunted them hard and never lost track of the point of it. He liked to find birds, he liked to shoot them, and he took pride in being very good at both. His chapters on recognizing likely grouse cover, wingshooting, hunting with and without dogs, and choosing guns and other gear remain as fresh and practical as they were 35 years ago when he wrote them.

Grouse hunting is hard work. Frank liked that. It's what made it worthwhile. "You will hike the birch woods and struggle through junipers and bull-brier, breast laurel jungles and scrub oak thickets," he wrote. "You will pause to take a breather after steaming climbs to beech ridges and plateaus where mountain winds are keen in the pines and hemlocks. If you decide to hunt partridges, one thing is certain: you'll walk."

But "every grouse hunter is an incurable romantic," he wrote, "else he would not seek this bird above all others." Frank Woolner was surely a romantic. "Usually," he wrote, "during the final afternoon of a grouse-hunting season, I take pleasure in tracking a fast-flying pat with my shotgun and, instead of pressing the trigger, I grin crookedly and lower the piece. There is a secret satisfaction in this sort of thing. I am sure that nobody ever bears witness, and it really doesn't matter. In essence, I have ended the season on my own terms."

Frank was also an optimist. "So far as this great bird is concerned," he wrote, "the elements are seldom hostile. Ruffed grouse conquered their environment centuries before any white man appeared on these shores. They are profligate enough to survive the attentions of wild predator and man. They retreat before the artificial lava flow of steel and cement, but they never concede victory while any fringe of woodland remains. If in the end of it, any game bird graces our wild lands, it will be the cocky, self-assured, and completely independent partridge of the north."

Developments in the 35 years since he wrote *Grouse and Grouse Hunting* might have tempered Woolner's optimism. These days the peaks in grouse population cycles barely reach what were, in his best days afield, the valleys.

Certainly highways and housing developments have stolen habitat from the ruffed grouse. But biologists tell us that the greatest threat to healthy grouse populations is not the bulldozer or the chainsaw, and certainly not the man with a shotgun.

Grouse thrive in the tangled edges where woods meet fields. There they find shelter from their enemies and the grasses, grains, leaves, and berries that make up their varied diet. The 19th-century New England farmers cleared the land, and when Frank Woolner began hunting grouse, he found the abandoned orchards and grapevine tangles, the old pastures grown to clumps of juniper and thorn-apple and edged with briar and brush, the cellarholes, graveyards, and stonewalls, and the second-growth birch and poplar hillsides that the pioneers left behind. It all made perfect grouse cover, and the birds were thick.

Today, in spite of the encroachments of civilization, New England actually boasts more woodland than it did a century ago. The problem is that it's rapidly reverting to mature forest. Tall trees and a open shaded understory make for poor grouse habitat.

If he would shoot predators to save grouse, Frank surely would have approved of the pro-active approach of the Ruffed Grouse Society, which promotes selective clear-cutting to let the sunshine into the forest and create the openings and thick edges that attract grouse, thus inten-tionally mimicking what the settlers created inadvert-ently a century ago. "To be entirely effective in this highly technical age," he wrote presciently, "successful grouse management may have to be a massive undertaking— and an expensive one. Perhaps a development of forestry practices that will benefit timbermen and hunters alike is one possibility. This is no dream, and it may be realized in the foreseeable future. The knowledge acquired by game biologists in their trysts with failure will be put to good use as natural resources practices mesh for the common good of mankind."

Those of us who savor Frank Woolner's words and love the woods in the fall and thrill to the roar of the sudden flush can only hope that his plea for intelligent management of grouse habitat will be heeded.

"There is time!" he wrote in 1970.

Let's hope he was right.

Chapter 11

WOOLNER'S
TIMBERDOODLE!

When I was much younger than I am now, I asked a grizzled old outdoorsman to tell me all about woodcock. He rubbed his chin and gazed up at the sky. "Well," he said, "they eat worms, they whistle when they fly, and they migrate. That's about it."

"But," I persisted, "how do you find them?"

He squinted at me and shrugged. "Woodcock," he said, "are where you find 'em."

I figured the old buzzard was putting me on. But after decades of hunting woodcock, I've come to realize that he was telling me everything there was to know. Woodcock eat worms, migrate, and whistle when they fly; otherwise they are mysterious, elusive, and altogether entrancing.

Nobody understood this better than Frank Woolner.

Those of us who have made their acquaintance know woodcock to be a peculiar, private, funny looking, and altogether lovable little birds. Aside from serious ornithologists, a few dedicated biologists, and a small but passionate breed of peculiar, private, and lovable sportsmen like Frank Woolner, who hunt them in the fall with pointing dogs and double-barreled shotguns, few people have ever even seen a woodcock.

As Woolner writes, the woodcock is "a shorebird oddball that has forgotten its ancient origins and prefers thick, moist, brushy uplands to the aboriginal edges of the sea. It is a secret and retiring atom of life, so given to elusive comings and goings in shadowy woodlands and the dark of night that millions of Americans are unaware of its very existence."

This worries those of us who hunt them and love them. Americans everywhere write letters to their legislators and donate large sums of money to conservation groups when the population declines of gaudier, more public birds like eagles and bluebirds are documented. Widely hunted game birds such as quail, ducks, and ruffed grouse have their own well-funded and politically savvy organizations dedicated to their preservation. Woodcock, meanwhile, cling to the coattails of the Ruffed Grouse Society, primarily because they share the same habitat and have historically been a happy byproduct of grouse hunting.

Timberdoodle!, Frank Woolner's book on the subject, covers just about everything anyone would want to know about the American woodcock: how to spy on them during their passionate springtime mating dances, how to select and train dogs that will find them, how to choose a suitable shotgun, how shoot them (and how to fabricate an effective alibi when you miss), and how to cook them.

The book omits the most important current fact about American woodcock, however, and that's this: For the past 35 or 40 years—roughly the time period since *Timberdoodle!* was first published—woodcock numbers have been declining at the steady and terrifying rate of 5 percent per year. The culprit, according to the experts, is loss of habitat.

In part, of course, it's the inexorable spread of civilization, the bulldozing and paving of the landscape that unselectively destroys the habitat of all wild creatures. Woolner knew all about this, and he railed against it. "If you're a cynic," he wrote, "the law seems to declare that biological ecosystems must be maintained—*unless* the destroyer files a plan that documents their proportion of destruction and promises to make amends. Having prepared such a blueprint, the developer may then tear the living earth apart, divert its streams, drain its wetlands, fill swamps, and kill all flora and fauna thereon. The paranoid assumption is that nature will not be affected, even though gravel, tarmac, cement, and steel replace peat bogs and alders."

Good woodcock cover is tangly, shadowy, and boggy. It's not good for much except harboring woodcock, and since most people wouldn't recognize a woodcock if they saw one, they tend not to value the bird's habitat or see much purpose in preserving it. Thirty-five years ago, the spread of gravel, tarmac, cement, and steel appeared to be the main threat to the prosperity of woodcock, and Woolner's tempered optimism made sense.

But the encroachments of civilization turn out to be a relatively minor factor in the loss of woodcock cover. Forest-fire prevention policies, restrictions on logging practices, and well-meaning but misinformed efforts to preserve rather than manage wilderness have combined to produce mature forests with high, thick canopies that prevent sunlight from reaching the ground. The rich mixes of hard and soft woods, bushes, briars, weeds, and vines that blanketed the New England landscape half a century ago are giving way to tall, homogeneous forests. Without brushy understory, sun-drenched open patches, and thick, tangly edges, woodcock and myriad other species are left without shelter, forage, and nesting grounds.

Adaptable species such as ruffed grouse are suffering, but they're hanging in there. Woodcock aren't particularly adaptable. Their needs are quite specific. Earthworms comprise more than 90 percent of their diet, and they must have soft boggy earth under their feet and low cover overhead. They simply cannot thrive in mature forests.

Had Woolner known of these developments, I have no doubt that he would have written a different book. This one is cheerful, quirky, optimistic, opinionated, and anecdotal, full of stories and debates about men and dogs, hits and misses, guns and recipes. "Nothing," wrote Woolner in 1974, "—not the clearing of lands, the guns of sportsmen, or the killing pesticides—has entered [the woodcock] on the lists of endangered species. He is prospering, still trading up and down the old flyways in spring and fall."

Alas, today the woodcock is not prospering. In this respect, you can read *Timberdoodle!* as a memoir of a happier, simpler era. Seasons and bag limits have been steadily reduced for both the Atlantic and the Mississippi flyways, but biologists agree with Woolner that men with guns are the least of the woodcock's problems.

Frank Woolner was a serious, albeit self-taught, natural historian and a passionate sportsman, and his love affair with woodcock glimmers in every word of this important book, which has been out of print for too long. He was born in 1916, lived his entire life in central Massachusetts, and died in 1994. He considered himself a political independent and a religious agnostic. Those of us who knew him can vouch for his straight-shooting Yankee independence. Read his words about woodcock and you'll understand that he was, in his way, a highly religious man. His cathedral was the outdoors and his pulpit was his writing desk.

When Frank Woolner came home from the Second World War in 1945, he became a full-time outdoor writer. He had no college education, so he learned his craft by reading, writing, and rewriting, and before he was done, he'd published hundreds of articles and several books on hunting, fishing, and nature. He wrote a weekly outdoors column for his local newspaper, and for 32 years he reigned as editor-in-chief of *Salt Water Sportsman.*

Although Woolner's name is most closely associated with surf fishing, he was, as were many sporting writers of his era, a generalist. He wrote as knowledgeably about wildflowers and tree frogs as he did about woodcock hunting and striped bass fishing, and he came by his knowledge first-hand. If you didn't find him at his typewriter, you knew he was outdoors, taking whatever the season offered. He fished for every species that swam in fresh and salt water, and he hunted every bird and animal that was legal. When nothing was in season, he tromped the fields and woods, looking, sniffing, listening, and learning. When he wrote about it, you knew he'd been there.

It would be a mistake to regard *Timberdoodle!* as just another how-to hunting book. Woolner doesn't even begin to discuss hunting until Chapter 6, and of its eleven chapters, only four are devoted to hunting and shooting. In "Black Powder Days," he gives us the best history I've read anywhere of the market-hunting era. "Say Grace!" contains tried-and-true woodcock recipes from hunters and their wives (including my mother). The balance of the book is natural history, a well-considered mixture of Woolner's own observations and those of fellow hunters, game biologists, and other writers.

He devotes an entire chapter to the charming courtship ritual of the woodcock. I have reread it dozens of times, and I always get a tingle. It's simply as good as outdoor writing gets.

Listen: "Never have I been close enough, or had hearing acute enough, to catch the soft, gurgling note that biologists say precedes the peent, but I watch my springtime friend strut back and forth, beak down and very proud of himself. His movements are vaguely reminiscent of the shorebird clans: he bobs when he walks, like a flesh-and-blood toy. He buzzes at intervals. Suddenly he flushes, flying low and fast for 50 or 60 feet before spiraling upward. Up, up—to a dizzying height where my glasses catch him again, hanging on fluttering wings some 200 to 300 feet above the somber, winter-killed earth, etched against the deepening blue gray zenith and the white sparks of stars. At flush, even my old ears have caught the wild twitter of wings, a sound that every upland gunner of eastern America will carry to his grave as a touch of paradise previewed."

Timberdoodle! is an informative and entertaining book, certainly among the best ever written about the American woodcock. But more than anything else, it's a love letter from an incurable romantic to the elusive object of his passion. "It is unthinkable," Woolner concludes, "to contemplate a world bereft of woodcock. We need comings and goings in the cold springtime and the hectic flush of fall. I still envision timberdoodles etched against a full moon, even though I know that this is ridiculous—but is there any man of our company who wars against a dream? Love timberdoodle, but never take him for granted. Count him an easy mark at your peril. Protect him forever."

Amen.

Chapter 12

T'AIN'T FAIR

*"T'ain't fair to the birds," insists [my friend the taxidermist]. "With
a good bird dog, all a fella has to do is walk along till his dog goes on
point. Then he goes in an' shoots the bird. He has his gun ready an'
he can't miss—well, anyways he shouldn't. No fightin' the brush, no
bein' caught with your pants down when a bird flushes—hell, that
ain't even huntin'. That's just goin' out for a walk."*

—*Ruffed Grouse*, John Alden Knight, 1947

There are three ways to hunt ruffed grouse: with a good
dog, with a poor dog, and with no dog at all.

A good pointing dog makes grouse hunting easy. It's the
classic way universally depicted in paintings, and if you
believe the literature of the sport, it's the standard way.

The art and the stories come either from another era or
from a romantic notion of how it's supposed to be. Once
upon a time, New England grouse were abundant and
lightly hunted and naive. They sat tight for a pointing dog
and waited for men with shotguns to come along and kick
them up.

Nowadays, at least in my experience, dogs that can handle our skittish PhD grouse are scarcer than clean doubles in thick cover. In more than 40 years of upland hunting, I've shot over just three certifiably excellent grouse dogs: Corey Ford's Cider, Keith Wegener's Freebie, and Skip Rood's Waldo. All three dogs were old by the time I made their acquaintance, and my times in the woods with them were few.

Frank Woolner, author of the classic book *Grouse and Grouse Hunting*, put it this way: "I am tempted to say that a great grouse dog is less common than the Holy Grail, but this is patently unfair. I have not seen the Holy Grail in my lifetime, yet I have hunted with and admired a few wonderful grouse dogs. Very few."

My own limited experience with great grouse dogs makes my expertise on the subject suspect. On the other hand, I've hunted with enough fair-to-poor dogs to know the difference.

A really good grouse dog is smart and old. He makes mistakes when he's young, but he learns from them. He's born with a love of hunting and a sharp nose. For him, the most intoxicating smell in the world is that of a grouse. A good grouse dog wants desperately to point. It takes him a lot of trying and erring to figure out how to get the job done. The more arthritic he becomes, the better he hunts. He's slow and methodical. He recognizes likely cover, approaches it cautiously, stays in contact with his hunters, and points from long distance.

Men who have owned one of these special dogs all say the same thing: They were patient, they got lucky, and they count their blessings. Good bloodlines help, although champion field-trial genes don't necessarily make good grouse dogs.

Hunting with a great grouse dog is, as John Alden Knight's friend said, "just goin' for a walk." After decades of hunting behind poor dogs, I've discovered that going for a walk in the autumn woods with a good one is a treat, and if you shoot the way I do, it's plenty fair to the birds.

There are many species of poor grouse dogs, but they all have one thing in common: They do more harm than good. They hunt too close and too slow, so that the grouse flush before they can point them, and they miss a lot of birds entirely. Or, they range too far and too fast, in which case they're beyond sight and sound if they point—or, more often, they flush the birds out of shotgun range.

I've done a lot of grouse hunting with poor dogs, and I've tolerated them because, for better or worse, I like dogs, and because, for all their faults, even an otherwise terrible bird dog will occasionally find a wing-tipped grouse that's burrowed under a blowdown. I figure any dog that does that has earned his supper, although it suggests that keeping a good retriever at heel might be a better way.

I've owned poor dogs, and I've hunted with other men's poor dogs. The only advantage of hunting with my own poor dog is that I'm the one who gets to yell at him.

Some dogs, when they're young, show flashes of brilliance even though they generally behave poorly. A few of them eventually get it and become prized grouse masters. Sadly, most dogs never get it. There's no such thing as a mediocre, or average, grouse dog, although men who own poor dogs optimistically refer to them as okay.

I'd rather hunt with dogs—even poor ones—than no dogs at all. It *is* the classic way.

But many of the craftiest grouse seekers I've known preferred to hunt without dogs. Frank Woolner was one of them. William H. Claflin, Jr., who wrote two delightful, privately printed books on New England grouse hunting (*Partridge Rambles*, 1937, and *Partridge Adventures*, 1951), was another. Claflin wrote: "When I travel through partridge cover I prefer not to have a dog along. I guess the simple answer is I am more interested in partridges and the country they live in than I am in pointers or setters."

My old friend Burton L. Spiller, on the other hand, couldn't imagine hunting grouse without dogs. "I will concede to any man the right to hunt grouse in any legal manner he chooses," Burt wrote in his 1962 story "Half-Century Grouse," "but when he says that dogs, even good dogs, are a liability, I am forced to disagree. I couldn't begin to list in this space all the advantages afforded a grouse hunter by even a mediocre dog. But I will say this: A dog will find more birds than any man can possibly find alone, give him more shots, find dead or wounded birds that would otherwise be lost, and be the best companion with whom one ever went afield."

It should be noted that Burt Spiller's heyday was a time when grouse were plentiful and lightly hunted compared to today. It was easier to forgive a dog that busted a few grouse out of range and ran past others. There were always more birds, and they'd sit tight often enough that even a poor dog might point a few of them.

Burt Spiller was a forgiving man. When I hunted with him, we always had poor dogs with us, and he never complained.

For me, it's more complicated, because I have a hard time choosing between the dogs and the birds, and I'm greedy enough to want the best of both, however rare that might be. But these days, when every grouse is precious, I'm considerably less forgiving of poor dog work than Burt was.

I like to hunt alone, when there's no one to blame but myself. I have found that picking my way through birdy cover without a dog taps into something atavistic and important that's absent when dogs are doing the hunting for me.

Hunting without a dog is . . . *hunting*. I find myself thinking like a grouse, scanning the cover, imagining where a bird might be lurking, how close he might let me approach, which direction he'll choose to fly.

Still-hunting, without early warning signals from a pointing dog, keeps my primitive hunter-gatherer senses alert. I notice everything—the pecked apples under a gnarled old Baldwin, the drill holes of woodcock in the mud, the flick of a squirrel's tail in the trees, the rustling in the dry leaves that might be a grouse.

I'm always ready for that sudden, explosive flush. I carry my shotgun at port arms, and I watch where I step. I expect grouse to do the unexpected.

I move slowly and quietly, hoping to sneak up on them. The ultimate still-hunting thrill is to spot a grouse on the ground or perched on a stone wall or in an apple tree before he sees me. Not that I'll shoot him. I won't, not unless he's flying. But still, sneaking up on an unsuspecting grouse is for me an unmitigated triumph, whether or not I end up killing it.

Ruffed grouse are survivors. Their senses are fine-tuned for predators. If they can elude hawks and foxes, the human predator, no matter how stealthy he is, rarely takes them by surprise. There are many kinds of noises in the woods. Grouse hear them all and can probably identify them, but I'm convinced that the sound of a man moving quietly and at a steady pace will not panic them. As long as they know where you are, they'll let you get close before they flush. Sometimes, in fact, they'll just sit tight and let you pass. The trick is to stop near a likely hiding place and remain still for a few seconds. When they lose track of you, they get nervous and flush.

Many seasoned partridge veterans—including Frank Woolner—have contended that jump shooting puts more grouse in the game pocket than hunting with dogs. I can't verify this, but I do believe that the jump shooter gets more good chances per bird flushed than everybody except that rare lucky fellow who owns a really good pointing dog.

More to the point, a man skilled at still-hunting can profit from his craft even when he shares the woods with a dog. As John Alden Knight wrote, "If you depend on a dog, or dogs, to find your grouse for you, you will miss a great deal of the pleasure that this brand of hunting has to offer. Aimless, painless wandering through grouse country in the wake of a good dog unquestionably will get birds for you; but if you plan your hunts and find your birds with the *incidental* help of a good dog, not only will you have better shooting but you will get more fun out of it."

Chapter 13

WHAT'S THE POINT?

Keith and I were following the edges of a tongue of thick cover that divided two old pastures. Burt, my Brittany, was working the tangly stuff between us. Suddenly Burt stopped, hesitated, then began tiptoeing. His stubby tail was a blur. "Dog's birdy," I called. "Roading a grouse, if I'm not mistaken. Be ready."

A moment later, the grouse spurted noisily but unseen out of the tip of the thicket, far ahead of us. Burt heard it, raised his head, thought about giving chase, then kind of shrugged and returned to business.

A minute later he locked on point. "Get ready," I called to Keith.

I shouldered my way into the thick cover. Burt's nose was quivering. Another step, and the woodcock flushed. My gun came up, but the bird was flying low, heading Keith's way.

He shot twice.

Then a second woodcock whistled up and angled away to my right. By the time I swung in its direction, it was just a flicker in the leaves. I shot at the flicker. An instant later I saw the bird above the treetops, flying hard, already out of range.

"Well?" I called.

"Nope. You?"

"Me neither."

Four other woodcock had settled into this 10-acre patch of cover. Burt pointed each of them. Keith and I missed them all.

When I caught up with Keith, he was rummaging in the pocket of his hunting vest. "At this rate I'm gonna run out of shells." He looked at me. "You notice anything peculiar?"

I shrugged. "Burt was pretty damn good."

"How many shots did you take in there?"

"Not sure," I said. "Guess I wasted five shells. Maybe six."

"Me too."

"Well, hell," I said. "That's not worth noticing."

"So what's your excuse?"

"No excuse." I shrugged. "I'm a pisspoor wingshot, I guess."

"What about the foliage? Kinda thick for good shooting. Wasn't the sun in your eyes or something?"

"Nah. Lousy shooting, that's all."

He nodded. "Exactly my point. No excuses. No complaints. I remember when you'd cuss and scream whenever you missed, which was quite often, as I recall."

"So did you."

"Sure I did. So what's the matter with us?"

"Matter?" I said. "Nothing. I'm having a pretty good time, myself."

"Precisely," said Keith. "A bunch of easy chances, not a feather in my pocket, and I'm sitting here thinking, hey, this is perfect."

"Well," I said, "it's close to perfect, though I suppose I'd like to reward Burt's points now and then with a dead bird, just to remind him of what it's all about."

Keith arched his eyebrows at me. "So what *is* it all about?"

When old Bucky died—hard to believe it was 20 years ago—I couldn't bring myself to replace him right away. I kept telling myself I should get a new dog, but one year stretched into a dozen. During that dogless time, many October and November weekends came and went and my shotgun stayed in its case. I left it up to Keith, Skip, Art, and other friends who owned bird dogs to invite me to hunt with them. If no one called, I didn't go.

When I didn't go, I missed it. Driving past an autumn field bordering an overgrown orchard, or a golden hillside sprouting head-high poplar and birch, or a meandering valley of alder along a woodland brook—those sights never failed to stir old longings.

But not hunting did not burn a hole in my stomach. I had plenty of good memories; maybe a lifetime's worth. They sustained me through those New England autumn weekends when I stayed home, and a few outings a season were enough to keep me going for another year.

When I thought about it, it worried me. I'd seen it happen to men of my father's generation. The loss of the hunting urge seemed, in them, like the natural progression of things. Their dogs got old. So did they. And their fires died. Hunting, they said, was too strenuous, took too much energy, left them too lame the next day. Anyway, they'd already shot a lifetime's worth of birds, and it wasn't anything like the good old days, when a man couldn't possibly feel guilty about harvesting a limit of grouse or woodcock.

I could never figure out if this was their rationalization, and if it was, what exactly they were trying to rationalize. But when I felt it beginning to happen to me, it just seemed as if some vital element in my soul was slowly bleeding away, the way, I'm told, the sex drive or the burning need to accumulate money eventually dries up. When it's gone, you don't even miss it.

I still liked to hunt, but I was beginning to understand that I could live without it.

It's possible that I might have gradually arrived at the point where I stopped hunting altogether—not because I'd weighed the costs and benefits of hunting and found the costs too high or the benefits too few, but simply out of inertia.

Then Burt joined the family.

The little Brittany was 8 weeks old and about 10 pounds of sniff and wiggle, a surprise birthday gift from my wife. I named him "Burton L. Spiller's Firelight," after my old friend.

He sight-pointed a moth the July afternoon that I brought him home. He was pointing the pheasant wing I'd strung from the tip of an old fly rod before he was house-broken. That first summer, Burt pointed the quail that Marty Connolly scattered in the weeds for him, and I held him steady on a check cord. I tried to train him according to the books. It wasn't hard. He quickly learned to *come*, to *heel*, to *whoa*, to *sit*, to *stay*. And I modified the normal command of *kennel* to *get-in-the-car*.

By September, I was eager for the hunting season—more eager, I realized, than I'd been in years. I believed I had a prodigy. Burt, I knew, had a terrific nose. He loved to hunt. He loved to please me. I couldn't wait to see how he'd handle wild birds.

When the first of October rolled around, he was 2 weeks shy of 5 months old. He was about the size of a long-legged beagle. Just a pup.

My hunting log for that season reminds me that we hunted with Keith and Freebie, his old setter, on Opening Day. We found the woods tinder-dry. The leaves had barely started to turn, and the trees had not started to drop them. The woodcock flights had not arrived. We bumped just three—and no grouse—from our good covers, shot none, and got no points, even from the veteran Freebie. Burt snuffled around. He seemed to ignore Freebie, though I had the feeling he was watching the old dog out of the corner of his eye. He appeared to be hunting. He obeyed my commands well enough. But as far as I could tell, he never got a whiff of a woodcock.

Art Currier and I hunted with Marty Connolly the following Saturday. Marty promised he could show Burt where some woodcock were hiding, and he was as good as his word. Burt's first woodcock points came that day, and that was when he introduced me to his version of retrieving. First he pointed a dead bird that had landed in a juniper. The second bird we shot he found, flash-pointed, thought better of it, and stood over it protectively until he knew I could find it. Then he wandered off to find another.

A little later, when Art wing-tipped a woodcock, Burt pinned it gently to the ground with his paw until I picked it up.

A few days later we hunted with Skip Rood and Waldo, Skip's wily old Brittany. Waldo was a legend. Those who'd hunted with him called him "Waldo the Wonder Dog." He was 14 years old and stone deaf, but his nose was still sharp, and his instincts were well-honed by years of experience. I figured Burt could learn something from Waldo, as he'd seemed to from Freebie.

That was the day he swam out into the middle of a pond to fetch the grouse Skip had shot. Later, he and Waldo doubled up on a grouse that they'd trailed for about 100 yards.

I hunted as often as I could that first season. I hunted more than I had in the previous four or five seasons combined—every weekend plus a couple of weekday after-noons each week. When the season ended, I took Burt to some private hunting preserves. I wanted to fill his nose with bird smells and to fill the air with rocketing game birds and the sound of shotguns and the smell of gun-powder.

And thus it has been since Burt came into my life. We hunt hard in the fall. In the spring, we hunt—without shotguns—for migrating woodcock that he can point. We hunt or practice hunting all year round.

Burt, it turns out, isn't quite a prodigy. He's awfully good, though. And he loves to hunt. The appearance of my hunting boots or shotgun case sends him zooming to the back door, where he sits expectantly, whining and panting. I love his enthusiasm. It's contagious.

Maybe I've reached the point in my life when I don't need to hunt, but I have accepted an obligation. I owe hunting to Burt. It's what he lives for. Hunting drives him and fulfills him. Poets must write, artists must paint, and bird dogs must hunt birds.

Yes, I hunt because my father hunted, and my father's father before him, and for all those other complicated psychological, cultural, genetic, and personal reasons.

But these days, more than anything, I hunt for Burt.

Keith and I worked our way down an alder-studded slope when Burt pointed again. I whistled to Keith, waited for him to get into position for a shot, then stepped in front of the dog.

The woodcock rose from under his nose and beat its way straight up to the top of the thick alders. I shot without thinking, and the bird crumpled and fell.

"Git 'im?" called Keith.

"Yep."

"Bout time."

I found Burt standing over the dead bird. I picked it up, smoothed its feathers, and held it down for Burt, who gave it a cursory sniff and wandered away.

Keith came over, and we broke our guns and sat on a log.

"A ways back there," I said, "you were asking what it's all about. How we could enjoy ourselves hunting when we weren't shooting a damn thing."

He shrugged. "It's a mystery, all right."

"Well," I said, "I think I've figured it out."

"I'm not sure I want to know," he said. "I like mysteries."

"Tough. Listen. In the beginning, men trained and bred dogs to hunt for them. Hounds to chase, terriers to dig, flushers to flush, pointers to point, retrievers to retrieve. The dogs' job was to find game so men could kill it and bring it home to eat. You with me so far?"

Keith smiled. "Hangin' in there."

"So," I continued, "Burt's job is to hunt for me. To sniff up birds and point them so I can kick them up and shoot them." I poked Keith's arm. "Remember how Freebie always pointed a woodcock in that corner just over the stone wall at Stick Farm, and how you got such a kick out of predicting it?"

"She was something, all right," said Keith softly.

"How would you have felt about walking into that corner without Freebie and kicking up that woodcock and shooting it?"

He shrugged. "Wouldn't've bothered doing that. No point to it." He chuckled. "Pun intended, come to think of it."

"Exactly," I said. "So Freebie might've been trying to find birds for us, but . . ."

"But," he said, "the fact is, we were trying to find birds for her. When I went hunting, it was as much for Freebie as it was for me."

"So that's it," I said. "That's what it's all about. That's why shooting and missing really doesn't bother me anymore. Burt doesn't seem to care one way or the other, as long as he gets to point them. And if he doesn't care, I don't, either. Now when I hunt, it's for Burt."

Keith cupped his hand around his ear. "Speaking of Mr. Burt," he said, "I don't hear his bell."

I listened. The woods were silent. I stood up, picked up my shotgun, and slid in two shells. "Let's go find him," I said. "If I'm not mistaken, we got ourselves another point."

Chapter 14

THE OLD COUNTRY

Every time Nick saw Doc, he was surprised by how small his old friend had become.

As usual, Doc was slumped in his chair beside the window. Elizabeth had spread a faded old crocheted afghan over his lap. The old guy's chin rested on his chest, and he was snoring softly. His skin was papery, his white hair thin and sparse.

Elizabeth gripped Doc's shoulder and gave it a gentle shake. "Wake up, dear," she said. "Nickie's here."

Doc's eyelids fluttered open. "I wasn't asleep," he said. "Just resting my eyes." He looked up at Nick. "You been hunting, I hope?"

Nick nodded.

Doc patted his leg, and Buck, Nick's 10-year-old Brittany, hobbled over and plopped his chin on Doc's thigh. Doc reached out with his left hand—his good one—and gave Buck's muzzle a scratch. "How many grouse did you point today?" he asked the dog.

"No grouse points," Nick told him. "We had three or four wild flushes. Never saw a feather." He dragged a chair beside Doc and sat down. "He pointed every woodcock we found, though."

"How many?"

"Five."

"Five woodcock? You hunted all day for five woodcock?"

"It's early," Nick said. "The flights aren't down yet."

Doc shook his head. "Even so . . . "

"I know," Nick said. "It's not like the old days."

"How many'd you shoot?"

"Two. The foliage is still thick. I was lucky to hit two."

"You're lucky to hit anything," Doc said. "I never saw a boy shoot so often and hit so little." He rubbed Buck's silky ear between his thumb and forefinger and cocked an eyebrow at Nick. "You remember that time we found Timbertop full of woodcock?"

Nick smiled and nodded.

"You must've wasted a box of shells."

"Close to it, I guess," Nick said. "Didn't touch a feather. I was only 13. The law of averages has been working in my favor ever since."

Doc didn't bother telling the rest of it—that he was five for five, a woodcock limit in those days, that October afternoon. Thirty-five years had passed since that day.

Doc shook his head. "I can remember every minute of it; every bird, every point, every shot. I can remember the angle of the sun and the smell of the woods and the feel of the mud under my boots and the sound of whistling woodcock wings." He looked over at Elizabeth, who was sitting on the sofa. "Remember that day, dear?"

"I wasn't there," she said. "You know that. It was you and Nickie."

"Of course I know that," he said. "I meant, you remember me telling you about it?"

Elizabeth smiled. Doc told the Timbertop story every Sunday evening when Nick stopped in to report on his weekend hunt. Sometimes he told it two or three times.

"So how many grouse did old Buck point for you today?" he said to Nick.

"None. I already told you that."

Doc shrugged. "I guess you did. Sorry. I don't know what's worse, living in a chair, or not remembering what you said five minutes ago. I can remember 50 years ago like it was yesterday, but five minutes ago is a blur."

Doc and Elizabeth more or less adopted Nick when his dad didn't come home from the hospital. They were middle-aged and childless, and Doc and Nick's father had been hunting and fishing partners. In a way, each of them filled Nick's dad's boots for the other: Nick became Doc's new partner, and Doc became Nick's new father.

In the winter they chopped holes in the ice and jigged for yellow perch. In the spring Doc took Nick to Sebago and Moosehead to troll streamers for landlocked salmon. After the snowmelt ran off, they fished for trout in local streams. In the summers they prowled the shorelines of lakes and ponds all over New England in Doc's canoe, casting Jitterbugs for bass and Dardevles for pickerel.

And every October and November from the time Nick was 12 until Doc had his first stroke, they spent weekends in what, even in those days, they called "the old country," the vast sprawl of alder thickets, river bottoms, birch and poplar hillsides, and abandoned pastures and orchards, all crisscrossed with dirt roads and stone walls, that lay in the shadows of New Hampshire's White Mountains.

Doc would toot his horn outside Nick's house at 7 on Saturday morning, and when Nick stumbled out to the car, Doc would be sitting in the passenger's seat. Nick learned to drive when he was 12. He guessed he must've logged 25,000 miles on Doc's Ford wagon before he was old enough to get his license.

While Nick drove, Doc told him stories about his father. Nick figured at the time that Doc was making sure he didn't forget his dad. He supposed it was also Doc's way of not forgetting him. Mostly they were hunting and fishing stories.

On Saturdays they hunted the covers—Doc and Nick's dad called them their "string o' pearls"—that took them northwards: First Chance, Black Alder, Bullring, Crankcase, Red Bloomers, County Line. They stayed in the Valley Hotel on Saturday nights. Doc's bird dog—first Bing, then Trip, then Duke—joined them in the hotel dining room. The dog lay at their feet under the table, and they dropped meat scraps to him. The management of the Valley Hotel welcomed bird hunters.

The last time Nick drove past the Valley Hotel, he noticed that the sign over the door now read "White Mountain Bible Center." He'd never mentioned that to Doc.

Their Sunday covers took them in an arc that ended up pointing southward, to home: Bonanza, Tripwire, The Old Hotel, Mankiller, The Treacherous Road Bird, Timbertop.

When they hunted together, Doc liked to recollect how he and Nick's dad had discovered each of those covers, how they got their names, how some birds were killed and others were ingloriously missed, how the dogs pointed and retrieved and got porcupined in them. Doc had a lot of memories of the old country, and in the years they hunted together, he and Nick added more to his storehouse.

They hunted grouse and woodcock in those New Hampshire covers for more than two decades. Then Doc had his stroke, and that was it. Nick stopped hunting in the old country. He found some covers closer to home and a couple of companions to share them with, and he left Timbertop and Bonanza and the rest of their old New Hampshire covers to Doc and his father and their memories.

Doc hunted vicariously now, trapped in his chair, his shriveled legs covered by his old afghan, stroking Buck's head with his good left hand while Nick told him his stories. It had been 15 years since Doc's first stroke, and Nick hadn't missed an autumn weekend in the woods in all that time.

The truth was, New England bird hunting was nothing like it had been when Nick was a kid, full of passion and energy, prowling the old country with Doc. There were too many hunters now, too many paved roads, houses, and gas stations. There also weren't enough birds, and for many years Nick had been feeling pangs of regret every time he shot a grouse or woodcock. He could easily have stopped hunting altogether.

But Nick figured he owed it to his old friend. If he were to stay home when it rained, or when he had a cold, or when he just didn't have the urge, Doc would miss out on a weekend's hunting.

So Nick went hunting, and he and Buck faithfully visited Doc and Elizabeth every Sunday evening in the autumn to report on the hunt. Thus they keep their partnership alive.

Elizabeth poured each of them a glass of red wine. It was Doc's medicine, doctor prescribed. In the old days, his drink of choice after a day's hunting was bourbon and branch.

Doc lifted his glass in his left hand. "To Mr. Partridge and Miss Timberdoodle," he said, as he always did. "May they prosper."

They clinked glasses, then sipped.

"So," Doc said, "start at the beginning."

When Nick first began to summarize his weekend hunts for Doc, he recited the numbers—birds started in each cover, points, shots, kills—but Doc quickly put him straight. He wanted to know what the birds were eating, what type of cover Nick found them in, how the woods looked and smelled, whether he saw any spawning brook trout in the streams. Doc was greedy for details, and Nick soon learned that he wanted stories, not just facts.

"Our first stop was at Buck's leg-stretcher," Nick said. "The goldenrod was thigh-high, not yet frost-killed, and the whole meadow glistened with dew in the slanting early sun. It was like walking through a field of diamonds. Buck headed straight for the alder run along the far side. I had to hurry to keep up with him. I figured it was still early in the season for flight birds, but sometimes a grouse scuttles down to the evergreen thicket at the end, and Buck knows it . . ."

Doc's eyes were closed, and he didn't interrupt, which told Nick he was telling it right.

Nick closed his eyes, too, visualizing the scenes, remembering the details, groping for the words to reconstruct it all for Doc. He recalled the moose tracks by the brook. When he'd spotted them, he thought how he had to fix it in his mind so he could tell Doc. He remembered how the Baldwin apples blanketed the ground in the old orchard on the sunny hillside, how some of them had been pecked, and how sweet they smelled when he crushed them under his boots. He remembered picking one off a tree and taking a bite—it was so sour it puckered his mouth—because he wanted to be able to tell Doc how it tasted.

And Nick was struck, as he was every Sunday evening in the fall, with how rich and intense his hunting experiences had become since he accepted the responsibility of recounting them to Doc. He noticed everything, and he evaluated its significance, and he filed it all away.

When he finished, Doc sighed and opened his eyes. "We had a pretty good day," he said. "Didn't we?"

Nick nodded. "We had a very good day. Every day in the woods is a good day."

"One of these days you should head over to the old country," Doc said, as he did every Sunday evening, "show old Buck our string o' pearls. Timbertop, Tripwire, Crankcase, County Line . . ."

Nick took a sip of wine and shrugged.

Doc nodded. "I know. They're probably all grown up, peppered with No Trespassing signs, bulldozed for house lots."

"I could check them out," Nick said.

"No," said Doc. "Leave 'em be. I like the way we remember them. Did I ever tell you how your daddy and I stumbled onto Bonanza?"

Nick smiled. "Many times."

"It was the third weekend in November," Doc said, "one of those slate-colored days when the air is chill and damp and you wouldn't be surprised if it snowed in the afternoon. Your dad and I were driving an old dirt road we'd traveled a hundred times, but on this particular day . . ."

Nick slumped back in his chair and closed his eyes. One of these days, he thought, perhaps he would sneak over to the old country, send Buck through Timbertop and Bonanza, if he could find them. He guessed he wouldn't tell Doc about it, though.

Chapter 15

THE CHIPMUNK HYPOTHESIS

Whenever a long day of chasing pointing dogs through Mankiller, Hippie House, Stick Farm, and our other grouse covers leaves our gun barrels clean and our game pockets empty, Keith and I don't blame our bird-finding skill or our luck or our dogs. Instead, we comfort ourselves with this handy explanation: The cycle must be down this year.

And when the other members of our New England grouse-shooting network also report slim pickins, even taking into account the Machiavellian secretiveness of partridge fanatics (we do not necessarily trust each other), we deduce a trend.

If the reports are consistently grim throughout the season, we assume we know why. Grouse populations are cyclical—always have been, always will be. Some years are better than others, and there's nothing you can do about it except wait it out.

I know that tromping through the same string of covers behind mediocre bird dogs for six autumn weekends a year is not the most scientific method for sampling the ruffed grouse population, but we keep careful count of the birds we flush, we do not count second starts, and we do it conscientiously year after year. So do our friends. We notice patterns. And the patterns we find generally seem to match those observed by the others who hunt grouse in New England—and even in other regions.

For most of my grouse-hunting life—close to half a century and counting—our No. 1 topic of discussion and concern has been population cycles. Up or down this year? Are the peaks really getting shorter and the valleys deeper? What causes them, anyway?

Theories abound: weather, predators, sun spots. No partridge man would be caught dead without a theory.

Of course, we have always been aware that the implacable loss of good habitat—highways, shopping malls, and housing developments, sure, but more importantly the maturing of the New England woodlands—is taking its steady toll. But that doesn't account for those ups and downs that keep coming regularly and predictably, the long, slow rise in grouse numbers and then the abrupt decline.

In the high-cycle years of the good old days—I mean 30 or 40 years ago—we'd sometimes start 25 or 30 grouse a day, and you could forgive your dog for flushing a bird wild or failing to hold a point, because there would always be more birds, and a lucky shotgunner might shoot a four-grouse limit and not feel too guilty about it. Even mediocre-looking cover would hold some birds.

Grouse numbers haven't been what they used to be here in New England for many decades. There's just not much good habitat left. But Keith and I have some secret places that, in good years, produce enough birds to keep us happy. In bad years we worry whether they'll rebound.

It's hard to accept the fact that those 30-bird days are gone forever.

Even in those secret covers of ours, we'd had several lean seasons in a row, so I was feeling darkly pessimistic on Opening Day last October. Trying to interpret those grim numbers as a temporary valley in the cycle rather than a clear sign of the permanent demise of the ruffed grouse was beginning to seem like whistling in the dark. But as Keith and I drove through the crimson-and-gold New England countryside with our shotguns and birddogs in back, he was humming "A-hunting We Will Go" and drumming his fingers on the steering wheel.

"What're you so damn chipper about?" I finally asked.

"Opening Day, my boy," he said. "A brand-new season. What could be finer?"

"The prospect of scaring up a few birds would help," I said.

"Oh, it's gonna be good. Big partridge year. Cycle's up. Mark my words."

"What makes you think so?"

He turned and grinned at me. "Chipmunks," he said.

"Huh?"

He shrugged. "I've been seeing lots of chipmunks this summer, and where you find chipmunks, you'll find grouse. It's gonna be a good partridge year."

I snorted. "How do you figure?"

"Grouse and chipmunks. They go together. Lots of chipmunks mean lots of grouse. See?"

"Not really."

"Acorns, son."

"Of course," I grumbled. "Acorns."

Those who are seriously concerned about the health of grouse populations focus not on cycles, which are natural, and therefore acceptable, short-term phenomena, and which, by definition, include an upturn for every downturn. Nowadays, we worry about the long, slow, steady decline in ruffed grouse populations. Each downturn of the cycle seems to dip lower, while the ensuing upturn doesn't bounce back quite as high. Biologists blame it on habitat loss—suburban and industrial sprawl, the expansion of the highway system, to be sure—but especially the loss of the thick understory that makes prime grouse cover. As second-growth forests mature, this is happening all over the northern tier of states.

Habitat loss is measurable and understandable. It can also, at least in theory, be reversed. The Ruffed Grouse Society promotes selective clear-cutting as the most promising way of addressing this unhappy trend and restoring healthy grouse numbers.

But regardless of the long-term scarcity or abundance of grouse, cycles will continue, and they'll continue to be mysterious.

I read somewhere that ruffed grouse abundance in New England fluctuates on the same four-year cycle as Atlantic salmon, UFO sightings, German pork prices, plankton yields in Lake Michigan, and cheese consumption. The article offered the cautious thesis that some of these correspondences might not actually be coincidental.

Nowhere else have I heard of a four-year grouse cycle. Still, I am intrigued by the idea that the same forces that push up pork prices and cause people to see UFOs actually influence the reproduction and survival rates of grouse.

Even more interesting is the possibility that eating cheese causes grouse to multiply.

I've never met a serious grouse hunter who didn't notice, worry, and speculate about their beloved bird's erratic and dramatic population booms and busts. Duck, deer, and turkey hunters of my acquaintance don't seem to obsess on the fluctuations in the abundance of their chosen quarry. But for grouse hunters, it's always been a puzzling, endlessly fascinating year-to-year phenomenon.

Perhaps if duck hunters were more observant and kept the kind of careful records that grouse hunters tend to keep, they'd notice comparable cycles in duck populations. Biologists insist that grouse population cycles are no different from the fluctuations in the numbers of other wild creatures. All flora and fauna, in fact, experience cyclical ups and downs. Maybe the real difference lies in the kinds of people who love to hunt ruffed grouse. The fact remains: Grouse hunters are constitutionally unable to engage in significant conversations with each other without sharing and debating their theories on population cycles.

Of course, if there were a scientifically conclusive explanation, there would be no need for speculation, and much of what fascinates us about this mysterious bird would be taken from us.

John Alden Knight, the creator of the solunar theory, noted that the population ups and downs of ruffed grouse correlated with cycles of solar radiation. Burton L. Spiller, known and beloved as the Poet Laureate of the Ruffed Grouse, often cited the periodic appearance of snowy owls as a surefire predictor of a sharp decline in grouse numbers. Outdoor writer Dan Holland observed that grouse numbers seemed to fluctuate the same as those of rabbits, except that grouse populations crashed a year or two after rabbits declined.

For all I know, Keith is right. Maybe chipmunks and acorns and grouse numbers are synchronous.

Still, correlation is not the same thing as causation.

The cycle is not simply the rationalization of unskilled or unlucky hunters. The periodic rise and fall of grouse populations has been observed and studied for centuries. In 1721, grouse numbers had declined so dramatically in Quebec that the provincial governor outlawed shooting. In New Hampshire, the abrupt disappearance of birds was first observed in 1831. New York market hunters experienced a sharp downturn in grouse numbers after the Civil War, and since that time, biologists and others have observed, studied, and speculated on the phenomenon. Their research proves that grouse populations do fluctuate cyclically, regularly, and predictably.

In his book *Ruffed Grouse*, published in 1947, Knight speculated at length on the phenomenon of grouse population cycles. He noted that they occurred independent of region, quality of habitat, or weather. Cyclical crashes occurred in both England and America in 1933, and in New England and the Midwest in 1944. Knight's research showed that the cycles made one complete revolution every 8 to 14 years—11 years, on average—although within each cycle there were fluctuations and cycles within cycles.

Gordon Gullion, who devoted his life to the study of grouse and grouse habitat, put the cycle at 10 years and found, furthermore, that the population crashes came predictably on years ending in 2 or 3: 1933, 1943, 1952, 1963, 1973, 1982. Gullion conducted his studies primarily in Minnesota, but the latter three of those years provided me with some pretty grim grouse hunting in New England, too.

The graph of a grouse population cycle does not look like the classic bell-shaped curve. Rather, it describes a long, ascending slope followed by an abrupt descent. Grouse numbers increase gradually over the 10- or 11-year period, rising and falling erratically here and there, until they reach their peak. Then, in the short space of a season or two, they crash and start over.

But *why?*

Well, nobody knows. Keith's chipmunk hypothesis holds that grouse flourish in years when the oaks produce a heavy acorn crop (which, of course, nourishes both grouse and chipmunks). But as he explains it, it's not simply that grouse like to eat acorns. Abundant acorns, in other words, do not cause grouse to flourish. Rather, it's that oak and grouse—and chipmunk—cycles coincide. Good mast years are good grouse years, but there have to be other, unknown variables at work, too.

It's complicated.

Those of us who love ruffed grouse pay special attention to springtime weather. A wet, cold nesting season takes a harsh toll on newly hatched chicks. Perhaps such weather conditions occur cyclically, although the research hasn't proven it.

Diseases and parasites can create epidemics. Predators, of which grouse have many, can wipe out young broods. Hawks and foxes might ignore grouse and be content to hunt easy-to-catch cottontails as long as they are abundant. But when they've decimated the rabbit population, they turn to more challenging prey like grouse. That, at least, was how Dan Holland explained why grouse numbers plummeted a few years after those of cottontails.

Several turn-of-the-century studies attempted to isolate the key variable. They postulated, among other things, poaching, market hunting, forest fires, severe winters, wet springs, dry summers, ticks, foxes, goshawks, dispersal, and migration. A report from New York state, attempting to account for the crash of grouse numbers in 1906–07, speculated that "the best bet [was] an unhappy combination of the cold wet spring, the unusual abundance of predators, and an epidemic of some disease or parasite." The unlucky coincidence of several negative factors, in other words.

It's doubtful that a single variable can be pinpointed as the cause of grouse cycles. Nothing in nature works in isolation. Ruffed grouse are part of an infinitely complex web of relationships. Weather, predation, disease, food, habitat—and, yes, for all we know, sunspots, chipmunks, and cheese consumption—are all woven together. Each factor affects the others. Tug on one thread and the whole pattern changes.

If prime habitat promotes high grouse numbers, then a heavy population of grouse will attract predators, parasites, and diseases. As these enemies feed off grouse, their numbers will grow. And when they have virtually eradicated the grouse, they, in turn, will experience a sharp downturn in their populations. This leaves the surviving grouse free to start rebuilding their numbers.

It's nature's way of maintaining the vigor of the species. In times of disease, predation, or severe weather, the weak die while the fittest survive to pass their strong genes along to future generations. This is Introductory Darwin, and it works for grouse, owls, germs, and chipmunks.

It also works for trees. Gullion discovered that during the upswings of the Midwestern grouse cycle, winter birds fed heavily on the male flower buds of aspens. These buds,

Gullion surmised, provided especially nutritious and efficient forage for grouse, giving them the strength and health to evade predators, to survive harsh winters, and to procreate bountifully in the spring.

Gullion also concluded that when grouse turn from aspen to less nourishing food sources such as hazel, birch, and ironwood, they have to spend more time and expend more energy in feeding. This, he speculated, makes them more vulnerable to predators, parasites, disease, and weather. Fewer birds survive the winter to reproduce in the spring, and newborn chicks are weaker.

But why do these birds stop eating aspen buds? Gullion made an interesting discovery, which he suggested might explain the connection between what grouse eat and the fluctuations in their numbers. Trees have survival mechanisms, too. When aspens are stressed by overbrowsing, which occurs when grouse are abundant, they produce a chemical that grouse (and other creatures) cannot digest efficiently. But when grouse numbers decrease, the aspens are no longer stressed, so they stop producing their defensive chemical. And again, in the cycle of things, grouse resume feeding on them.

And so it goes. Cycles within cycles. It's nature's way. Hunters can resent it or admire it, and we can help grouse by supporting habitat improvement projects and research, but cycles will continue, and nothing will change that.

Keith pulled up to the gas pumps in front of a ramshackle mom 'n' pop store where two dirt roads intersected. A young guy wearing overalls and a black beard ambled out. He planted his forearms on the roof of our wagon, bent down, and peered inside. He saw two men wearing leather-faced pants sitting up front, one Brittany and one English pointer whining in back, and, on the floor, two 20-gauge doubles, several boxes of shotgun shells, leather boots, shooting vests, check cords, belled collars, and a wicker picnic basket.

He scratched his beard for a moment, processing the clues, and then grinned. "Bird hunting, eh? Well, lissen. You boys wanna know where you can find yerselves some pa'tridges?"

"Partridges?" said Keith. "The hell with partridges. We're looking for chipmunks."

Chapter 16

OUR POET LAUREATE

In the fall of 1955, when I was 15 and my father figured I was responsible enough to carry a shotgun in the woods, he made me his gunning partner. At that time, Dad's long-time grouse-hunting companion was an elderly man named Burton L. Spiller. We became a threesome. Every October and November weekend for the ten seasons that took me from adolescence to adulthood, Dad, Burt, and I followed pointing dogs through the alder runs, briar tangles, poplar hillsides, abandoned orchards, and stream bottoms that, as Burt described it, formed a corridor from Lake Winnipe-saukee in New Hampshire to Sebago Lake in Maine.

Burt was 69 years old when I met him. He was 78 in 1964 when a fall in the woods forced him to quit hunting for good. Today, I am the only man still alive who hunted grouse with Burton L. Spiller.

In the 10 years that I hunted with Burt, I grew to love the old guy. Our conversations were the casual kind you have with a hunting companion. Mostly they concerned the tactics and strategies of finding grouse and shooting (and missing) them. We discussed baseball, mainly the plight of the Red Sox, and the beauty of New England in the fall. Sometimes Burt told a gentle joke. We avoided heavy topics like business, politics, or religion. Hunting was more important.

In retrospect, given the direction my own life seems to have taken, I regret the fact that I never asked Burt about the writing life. I knew he wrote, of course. I'd read plenty of his stuff, and even as a kid I had enough sense to appreciate it. But I was more interested in hunting than writing.

In the time that I knew him, Burt was always working on a magazine story or a book. Altogether, he published seven books and hundreds of magazine articles and stories—53 in *Field & Stream* alone. Many others appeared in *Hunting and Fishing* and *Outdoors*, magazines that my father had edited. Many, but by no means all, of Burt's stories were about upland bird hunting.

A lifetime of labor at his old Oliver typewriter on the dining-room table in his modest white frame house in East Rochester, New Hampshire, earned Burton L. Spiller the unofficial title "Poet Laureate of the Ruffed Grouse." I suspect that if the only words he ever published were those that were contained in two books, *Grouse Feathers* and *More Grouse Feathers*, his legacy would be secure.

For those two books, Burton L. Spiller—and those of us who love his stories—can thank his editor, Eugene V. Connett. Kevin Shelly, a reporter and author who knew of my friendship with Burt and who was researching a book about Burt's illustrator, Lynn Bogue Hunt, generously shared with me the Spiller-Connett correspondence, which spanned the years 1933–1940. These old letters offer an intimate peek into the minds of both writer and editor and tell the story of Burt's four Derrydale books that were published, one a year, from 1935 to 1938.

Burton L. Spiller's very first grouse-hunting story, "His Majesty, The Grouse," appeared in *Field & Stream* in the fall of 1932. Burt was 46 years old, but just a beginning writer. The following June, he received this unexpected letter:

> *Dear Sir:*
>
> *I happened to read the second part of your story "His Majesty the Grouse" in* Field & Stream, *and I liked the way you wrote it, and the knowledge of the subject it evidenced.*
>
> *If you would care to think over the matter of writing a book on shooting, I would be glad to either talk to you about it in advance, or to give the manuscript very careful consideration when it is submitted.*

The letter was signed by Eugene V. Connett, president of the Derrydale Press, which was, at the time, the country's most prestigious publisher of sporting literature. It was the sort of letter that magazine writers dream of receiving, and Burt wasted no time replying to it. His delight at the prospect of publishing a book is disguised, but not entirely hidden, by his typically polite, diffident language:

Dear Mr. Connett:

Thank you for the tribute to my grouse story in Field & Stream *and the suggestion concerning the writing of a book on shooting. As it happens, I am very favorably impressed with the idea. In fact, I have been assembling material for several years with that object in view.*

What I had planned was a work taking up the various phases of grouse hunting and allotting to each a definite place in the story, illustrating each angle with an anecdote or two and enlivening the whole with humor of the repressed variety.

By that I mean treating the whole serious business (and to a vast army of scattergun enthusiasts it is a serious business) in a style similar to that which I used in His Majesty, the Grouse.

My material would, I think, carry the yarn through to almost any length you might require.

I wonder if this coincides with your conception of a shooting story. If you would write me at length concerning your requirements as to material, treatment, and length, I would be glad to start work at once and submit the manuscript for your approval.

Throughout their 8-year relationship as editor and author, Burt Spiller and Eugene Connett never met. There is no evidence that they even spoke on the telephone. They communicated by letter exclusively. In those 10 years, they never called each other by their first names.

Within days of receiving Burt's reply to his inquiry, Connett wrote:

Dear Mr. Spiller:

I think your suggestion for the outline of the grouse shooting book is very good. I hesitate to suggest how long the book should be, as I think that is a matter for an author—at least at the start. I don't want a padded book, nor one that is scimped [sic]. You will have about so much really important material and that is what should be used.

Would it be possible to include something on woodcock shooting in the manuscript? The two birds seem to go together as a rule, and the inclusion of woodcock might broaden the market for the book. Grouse shooting is a very local sport in terms of book sales throughout the whole U.S. You might think this over.

On July 24, Burt replied in longhand (and with his characteristic humor "of the repressed variety") that he would certainly include woodcock in the book and hoped "to be able to submit the mss. in about two months or, if you desire accuracy, just prior to the month of October, around which, on my calendar, is a large circle of vivid red." In fact, he didn't mail off the manuscript until December 28, 1933.

So far he had no contract or, in fact, any commitment whatsoever beyond the editor's promise to give it "very careful consideration."

Burt had to wait six months for Connett's response. That must have felt to the hopeful author like a very long silence. This, remember, was in the depths of the Great Depression, and publishers, like everyone else, were feeling the pinch. The decision to publish a book, especially one by an essentially unknown author, was not taken lightly, and we can only imagine the self-doubts and anxieties Burt must have felt while he waited.

Connett's letter was dated June 1, 1934:

Dear Mr. Spiller:

I certainly owe you an apology for having kept you waiting so long for some word about your book, Grouse Feathers. The real reason for the delay has been that we have been waiting to see how our spring books went and whether there would be an indication of improvement in business.

First of all, we like your book very much indeed, and want to publish it. But don't want to publish it while conditions are so bad. We find that it is not safe to publish anything but sure bets by well-established authors at present, and I think both you and ourselves will be much better off if we hold your book back until there is some life in the book business again.

When the time seems ripe I would like to make a beautiful limited edition with good illustrations to sell for about $7.50 a copy. I believe that is the best way to handle such a book as yours. Grouse *shooting is fairly localized in the northeastern states. Grouse shooters are great enthusiasts, and should appreciate a fine book on their sport. Therefore a limited edition, such as we usually publish, would be the proper thing in this case.*

Now, if you feel that you do not care to wait any longer, I will of course return the manuscript but I hope you will feel able to put up with a further delay for the reasons I give.

Let me repeat that I think very highly of the book; it is well written, interesting, and thoroughly authentic. I shall enjoy publishing it just as soon as business conditions warrant it.

Another six months passed. Then in January of 1935, Connett wrote to tell Burt that *Grouse Feathers* was scheduled for publication in the fall and that John Frost would be the book's illustrator. In June Connett sent Burt a contract along with the news that "Mr. John Frost has developed tuberculosis" and that the illustrating job would instead be done by Lynn Bogue Hunt, who "does some remarkably fine work privately." Now the plan was to publish the book at "about $20 per copy in an edition of about 750 copies." A month later Connett wrote that he had "about decided to make *Grouse Feathers* a $10 book," since $20 "does seem a bit rich for the book in days like these."

The book was published, appropriately, in October of 1935, and in December Connett wrote: "The book has been very well-received and the edition is sold out. Congratulations! Wishing you a happy New Year and looking forward to your next manuscript."

Throughout their correspondence, Burt peppered Connett with ideas for other books. Shortly after submitting *Grouse Feathers*, Burt told the editor that he had been "working on a book of animal stories," and less than a month after signing the contract, he sent Connett an unsolicited "manuscript of a little yarn in which I am firmly convinced there should be a future." Burt described it this way:

> The chief character, "Further Out Bill," is a composite character, drawn, more or less, from the lives of several acquaintances in whom the wanderlust was a primal urge that had to be gratified.
>
> Believing this inherited instinct burned as strongly in the breasts of most men, as any one thing bequeathed by our forbears, I conceived the idea of trying to capture the spirit of the thing.
>
> It is my belief that, if it could be published in a rather nice little gift book, to sell at a reasonable price, it would have a definite appeal to the multitude of men who still believe the far horizons are the fairest and that every rainbow has its pot of gold.

In late 1936, in a P.S. to a letter, Burt told Connett: "Have in mind a humorous baseball story. Would that be acceptable?" In early 1937 Connett proposed that Burt write a play about fishing, to which Burt responded enthusiastically and submitted a plot sketch. That summer Burt proposed "a fishing book done after the manner of *Grouse Feathers*" and also asked whether the editor would be interested in a novel he had finished called *Rainbow Gold*, which he described as "a business-adventure story—a he-man's yarn." Burt also queried the editor about "*a cheaper edition of Grouse Feathers,*" a compilation of newspaper columns devoted mostly to fishing, and an historical novel.

Burton L. Spiller was a writer, eager to get his words into print. Eugene V. Connett was a publisher, eager to produce books that would earn his house a profit. Given the success of *Grouse Feathers,* Derrydale published *Thoroughbred* in 1936 and *Firelight* in 1937. Both books were collections of stories mostly on outdoors subjects, but not necessarily about hunting. It was the editor's difficult duty to report to the author that both books were flops. In a letter dated July 21, 1937, replying to Burt's inquiry about the fishing book, Connett explained:

Dear Mr. Spiller:

I should be very glad to see a book like Grouse Feathers *on fishing.* Grouse Feathers *is a classic, but the two other books have not met with an equally enthusiastic reception, I'm sorry to say.*

I don't think the time is ripe for a cheaper edition of Grouse Feathers *because, to be entirely honest, your last two books proved a disappointment to so many of our customers.*

I should go on to explain that people who bought and liked Grouse Feathers *naturally expected to get something similar when they bought the next books, and we know that there is no similarity.*

It may be dumb on the part of book buyers, but when they get something they really like, they want more of the same sort of thing instead of something entirely different.

I knew all this when I published Thoroughbred *and* Firelight, *but I have been living in hopes that you would get back to the level you reached in* Grouse Feathers.

I regret exceedingly that we have never had a chance to talk together, as I could then explain to you the theory behind the publications of this Press. Books published at $10 per copy have to have a permanent value—their contents must be of sufficient weight and worth to withstand the years. They must be a real contribution to the sporting lore and literature of America. Grouse Feathers *had all this. The other two books were simply collections of unrelated stories—well written, but very ephemeral. They did not build up any particular significant characters in American sport—fictional or real. Nor did they make any significant contribution to the American sporting scene of today or yesterday as* Grouse Feathers *did.*

I hesitate to write thus to you, as you may take an antagonistic position which I couldn't combat through the mail—nor will I try to. If we were face to face, you could unburden your mind and I could explain in detail what I am driving at.

I hope that you will really try to follow me, so that we can get together for more books. Frankly, I can't afford any more like the last two; on the other hand, I'll publish as many Grouse Feathers *as you can write!*

I have the feeling that you do not visualize our market accurately. I believe I know the men who comprise it pretty well—else I would have gone out of business long ago. But I can't begin to tell you about it in a letter. I can only tell (fairly well) whether a MS will please it.

Now, fire all the questions at me you can think of. Unless you can develop some grand characters for your fishing book, I shall be surprised if it will do. But with significant characters and types carrying the burden of the fishing theme, it might be O.K. Please remember that everybody and his cousin has written about fishing (which was not true of grouse shooting) and it is much more difficult to write a classic about fishing for that reason. However, go to it, and count on me for honest criticism and all the help I can give.

Burt, characteristically, did not take an "antagonistic position" to Connett's candid words. He replied: "Thanks for your recent letter. It was so comprehensive a one that it has cleared up a number of points which were not clear to me." He said that he intended to pursue the fishing book and that he hoped to find a publisher for his historical novel.

On November 10, 1937, Connett wrote:

Dear Mr. Spiller:

Are you doing anything about another book, on the lines of Grouse Feathers? *People liked that book so much, that you could almost do another on grouse if you are short of subjects.*

I don't want a book on the lines of Thoroughbred *or* Firelight, *neither of which clicked very well. I do want a second* Grouse Feathers, *which was a grand success.*

Burt replied that the idea appealed to him "strongly," and wondered if "it would be safe to do one in the same reminiscent vein, with grouse as the central theme, but stepping aside occasionally to include some of the other bright spots in my shooting memories?"

Connett replied: "The chief thing I want is sporting stuff—no fire fighters and no more big game subjects for the time being."

On December 14, 1937, barely a month after Connett proposed the sequel to *Grouse Feathers*, Burt wrote:

> *Dear Mr. Connett:*
>
> *Here is the first installment of that new grouse book.*
>
> *As I have studied it, the thing somehow seems to divide itself into periods of sevens, and it occurred to me that the story might well be divided thus, trying always to get the true perspective of that particular period of my life, and finding out if possible what thing it is within one that makes him a grouse hunter.*
>
> *In going over* Grouse Feathers *again I find I didn't devote much space to dogs. I don't know why, for I am a crank on grouse dogs. I wish also to discuss guns a bit more, and I have learned a great many things about birds in the last year or two. I am quite certain I have ample material—if it happens to be of the sort required.*

Burt submitted the last chapter for *More Grouse Feathers* on February 5, 1938, and the book appeared in April to enthusiastic reviews and good sales.

For the next couple of years, Burt continued to submit book proposals. Connett, who was then ailing, accepted none of them. In 1940 he rejected the fishing book that the two of them had been discussing in a short note: "I'm afraid your new manuscript won't fit into our list. I enjoyed reading it and thank you for letting me see it."

Burton L. Spiller's historical novel, his "he-man's yarn" called *Rainbow Gold*, his "Further Out Bill" story, his volume of animal tales, his fishing play, his humorous baseball story, his collection of fishing columns—none of them appeared in print. A collection of fishing stories called *Fishin' Around* was published by the Winchester Press in 1974, the year after Burt's death at age 87. We'll probably never know if it was the same book that Eugene V. Connett declined to publish in 1940.

Chapter 17

VIRTUAL HUNTING

The sound of gunfire lured me into the living room where Ben, my step-son, was playing a video game. He was manipulating a complicated electronic device with both hands, and he was using it like a gun to shoot at figures on the television screen that darted out of doorways, sprang up from behind automobiles, and leaped down from rooftops. When he hit one, it screamed and exploded in a fireball. In the corner of the TV screen was a scoreboard that recorded his hits and misses.

As the game proceeded, the figures appeared more suddenly and moved faster. When Ben failed to hit them, they shot back at him. Mostly, he hit them. He was quick and accurate. Ben had never been bird hunting, but I guessed he'd make a pretty good wingshot.

This got me thinking: Suppose, instead of evil creatures bent on the destruction of the world, the figures on the screen were ducks, grouse, or pheasants. Suppose the shooter was hunched in a duck blind or moving through a cornfield or stand of second-growth poplar. Suppose a brace of virtual English setters quartered ahead of him.

Instead of a play station television game, you'd have one of those virtual-reality devices pulled over your head and a virtual shotgun in your hands. With the wonders of modern technology, they could make it look, smell, and sound real. You could hunt whenever you wanted for as long as you wanted without getting wet, cold, or tired. You could choose your birds, your dogs, your terrain. Just press the select button for Chesapeake geese, New England ruffed grouse, Argentina doves, or Africa mixed bag, hit the start button, and enjoy an afternoon of bird hunting from the comfort of your living room.

Virtual hunting. I can imagine the day when that'll be the only bird hunting we'll have.

I went quail hunting for the first time about 20 years ago. I'd never hunted anywhere outside of New England before. I'd never hunted quail. My friend Rick Boyer, who had recently moved to North Carolina, said I had to come down and do it, and I agreed. I'd been reading about Southern quail hunting all my life.

Rick booked us at a plantation in south-central Georgia for the last week in February. He picked me up at the airport in Atlanta, and we drove through the red-dirt countryside. It was springtime and the peach orchards were in blossom. We stopped at a roadside shack and ate authentic pulled-pork barbeque sandwiches at picnic tables.

I was pretty excited.

We had grits, eggs, ham hocks, and biscuits and gravy for breakfast. Then we waited in rocking chairs on the verandah for Lyle, our guide, to fetch us. The morning sun was warm on our faces; the air was sweet with the scent of flowers, pine needles, and damp earth, and robins were plucking earthworms from the lush lawn. Back home there were two feet of snow on the ground.

After a while, Lyle pulled up in his Chevy pickup. It had two dog boxes in the bed, a gun rack in the cab, and a tattered Confederate flag flying from the antenna.

We bumped over dirt roads past fields rioting in wildflowers and oak woods lime-green with new leaves. Lyle talked about auto racing, catfish farming, bird dogs, and Georgia football. He called us "sir," and when we asked him not to, he said, "Cain't he'p it, suh. It's how I was raised up."

After a while we stopped at a field. He called it a "course." It grew about knee-high in some kind of grass. There were patches of briar tangles and a few meandering game trails. The course was surrounded by brushy edges and scrubby oak-and-pine woods. It looked remarkably like the A. B. Frost print I've got hanging in my den.

Lyle let out the dogs while Rick and I pulled on our boots.

A minute later Lyle whistled, and when we looked up, we saw that one of his setters was on point near a clump of briars and the other was honoring her. It was classic, straight out of Nash Buckingham, and at that moment I felt somehow connected to the very roots of American bird hunting.

I'd seen bobwhite quail on Cape Cod, and heard them whistling toward evening and at dawn. I knew they gathered in coveys, and when they flushed, it would be a sudden explosion of what the stories called little brown bombshells. The trick, I remembered, was not to flock shoot.

Rick and I got our shotguns loaded. Lyle motioned for us to move into position on either side of the dogs. He'd go in and kick up the birds.

There were just two quail in that covey. One flew left, my way, more slowly than the stories had led me to expect, and the other went straightaway in front of Rick. I swung and shot, and my bird dropped. Rick dumped his, too. It was vaguely disappointing. I'd expected a dozen or more birds darting in all directions, the whirr and blur of two dozen frantically beating wings, pandemonium.

But it was southern quail shooting, and hey, I'd hit the first one I'd ever shot at over a classic point within minutes of arriving at the course. Not too shabby.

By the time we'd stuffed our birds into our game pockets, the dogs were pointing again.

Lyle kicked up two more quail. Rick and I dropped both of them, too.

A few minutes later it was a mini-covey of five birds. I shot a double. In a lifetime of hunting grouse in New England, I'd never doubled.

We followed the game trails (which were suspiciously littered with spent shotgun shells) through the grass-and-briar course while the dogs quartered ahead of us, and every 50 yards or so they pointed, Lyle kicked, and we shot. The birds came mostly in pairs, they flew straight, and Rick and I rarely missed.

When we came to the end of the course, Lyle muttered, "Twenty-two, right?"

"I wasn't counting," said Rick.

"Well, suh, I'm pretty sure we flushed twenty two," said Lyle. "We got us a couple more somewheres." He scratched his head for a moment, then nodded. "This way, gentlemen," he said.

We followed him to a corner of the course that we had missed. Lyle called over the dogs, and a minute later they were pointing again.

Two more quail in our pockets.

The man really knew his quail, I was thinking.

Back at the truck, Rick and I unloaded our game pockets and laid 19 birds on the ground. Lyle said we'd flushed 24.

I'd never shot more than five upland birds—a woodcock limit—in one day in my life. That had cost me almost a box of shells. Today I'd shot ten in three hours, and I still had a fistful of shells left from the box I'd dumped into my pockets.

Sometime around then I figured it out. When I did, I felt stupid and naive.

While I had been eating the first grits of my life that morning, Lyle was at our course planting the two dozen quail Rick had bought. He tucked the birds' heads under their wings and rocked them dizzy so they'd stay put, then set them out, a pair under this hummock of grass, another pair in this briar tangle, five under this shrub—the same places, no doubt, where he'd put them out the day before for some other pair of Yankee shotgunners.

Southern plantation hunting was the private, upscale equivalent of northern put-and-take public pheasant hunting—pen-raised birds and scientifically-managed terrain, all designed for the shooting enjoyment of anyone who could afford it.

Rick, of course, knew all this, and he'd assumed that I did, too. He knew that we were paying about $7 for every quail that was planted for us, whether or not we shot it. "We could have had chukars or pheasants," he said, "but they run $10 or $15 apiece. I figured we'd go for more bang for the buck."

It was a lot like learning that my father was Santa Claus, and I'd like to report that my disillusionment was so profound that I packed my bags and flew back into the New England winter.

But I didn't. I stayed the week and enjoyed the southern cooking, the southern hospitality, and the southern springtime. Seeing the dogs work was a treat and, of course, we did a lot of wingshooting. In the end, my disappointment that the quail weren't wild was more than offset by the knowledge that shooting dozens of them had no more impact on the fragile natural balance of things than buying a shrink-wrapped chicken in a supermarket.

Lyle told us that truly wild coveys of quail were so scarce and hard to find in the South these days that not many people hunted them anymore. When I told him that this plantation deal seemed kind of artificial, he shrugged. "In the old days," he said, "when the birds were wild, the plantation owners grew crops to feed them and cut and burned the fields and woods to make cover for them. They knew where all the coveys were, they only let their friends hunt them, and they made sure enough of them survived to maintain their numbers. It wasn't all that much different. They raised 'em for hunting back then, too. This here's what we got for quail hunting nowadays."

Here in the Northeast we call them preserves, not plantations, but it's the same deal. Pheasants, not quail, are the most popular bird, but they can put out chukars, quail, or Hungarian partridge if you want. It doesn't matter if the birds can survive in our climate. Their life's purpose is to be shot.

Once you understand how it works, it's impossible to conjure up the same stomach-clenching anticipation as when you wake up for a day of real hunting. On the other hand, this fake, designer hunting is not much different from fishing for hatchery-raised trout, and I've learned to call that trout fishing.

I imagine that one day they'll figure out how to breed domesticated strains of slow-flying ruffed grouse and non-migrating woodcock, hybrid birds that will sit tighter for a pointing dog and are easier to shoot than our clever native varieties. Dumber birds would make good economic sense: better return for investment; greater customer satisfaction.

They've already done that with pen-raised pheasants and quail.

Call it virtual hunting. It takes only a few minor adjustments in your thinking to call it, simply, hunting.

Until they come out with that video game, this is the future.

Chapter 18

OPENING DAY

*Fishermen, hunters, woodchoppers, and others, spending their
lives in the fields and woods, in a peculiar sense a part of Nature
themselves, are often in a more favorable mood for observing her, in
the intervals of their pursuits, than philosophers or poets even, who
approach her with expectation.*

—*Walden*, Henry David Thoreau, 1854

I went to bed at 10 PM and set my alarm for 2:15. I read for a while before I turned out the light, then I stared at the ceiling, waiting for the alarm to go off. I never sleep the night before Opening Day of duck season.

We called our secret pond Tranquility, after the book by Col. Harold Sheldon. We'd found it on a topographic map, where it had a different name. We'd followed the lumpy old tote road to Tranquility's muddy banks in Keith's 4WD truck and, yes, it was loaded with mallards, woodies, and blacks. They traded back and forth to the swamp over the hill at sunrise and again at dusk.

We'd had a lot of fun all summer, watching the ducks fly over our pond and anticipating Opening Day. Now it was upon us.

Tranquility is shallow, weedy, and mud-bottomed, the product of an ancient milldam on a little trout stream in the hills of southwestern Maine. We made countless trips across the pond in Keith's Old Town canoe to the site we'd chosen for our blind—on the tip of a point on the east bank, so the morning sun would rise behind us, with the head-high cattails at our backs. We loaded the canoe with plywood, 2 x 4s, stainless-steel stakes, and chicken wire, and we sweltered under August skies, up to our hips in water, to cobble our blind together. We paddled the creek channel so many times that its meandering course was imprinted on our brains, and we knew we could find our blind at 4 o'clock on a moonless October morning.

The streets were dark on the drive to Keith's house. I felt foolishly virtuous, being up and around while the rest of the world was squandering that magic time. The orange glow from Keith's kitchen window was a beacon in the night. I tapped softly on the back door, found it unlocked, and went in. The mingled, evocative aromas of frying sausage and perked coffee greeted me.

I sat at the table and Keith slid a mug of coffee in front of me. Raisin, his old brown Lab, shuffled over and plopped his chin on my knee. I scratched the special place on his forehead. He whimpered and thrashed his tail. He knew it was Opening Day, too.

We ate two-handed—a fork for stabbing hash browns and sausage, a biscuit for sopping up egg yolk. "Three-duck limit, you know," mumbled Keith. "Hardly worth it."

"That's how everyone else will figure it," I said. "They figure, buy a license, federal duck stamp, and state waterfowl stamp, then give up a night's sleep and a day's work for a lousy three ducks? It ain't worth it, they'll figure, so we'll have the birds all to ourselves. A three-duck limit sounds good to me."

"If they're flying," he said, "it'll be all over in the first 15 minutes."

"So?"

He nodded. "Valid point."

The moon had set, and except for a billion stars, the October sky was black when we got to Tranquility. We loaded our decoys, camouflage netting, shotguns, shotshells, Thermos bottles of coffee, and bags of donuts, then the three of us got into Keith's canoe, and we paddled across to the blind by starlight. Out of deference to the quiet, we were careful not to thump the gunwales with our paddles,. We could hear ducks gabbling softly in the potholes. They were all around us. Raisin whimpered, and I thought I heard Keith whimper, too.

By the time we got to the blind, the stars had started to blink out and the sky was turning sooty. We shoved the canoe under some bushes, and I began draping the netting around the blind, cutting some cattails and sticking them across the top to break our silhouettes. Raisin sat beside me, scanning the horizon.

Meanwhile, Keith was in his hip boots setting out the dekes. I looked up when I heard him whistle. A big flock of mallards came skimming over the blind, turned, and splashed into the decoys all around Keith. He quacked at them. They ignored him. Then he laughed, and the birds jumped and flew away.

We were all set up by 6 o'clock, a half hour before legal shooting. "We probably won't see any more ducks all day," Keith said. "Just those dumb ones that didn't even notice me muckin' around out there."

"They weren't that dumb," I said. "They knew it was too early to shoot."

Just then about a dozen black ducks materialized in front of us. They dropped into the decoys and noodled around for a while before they paddled off. A pair of wood ducks circled a couple of times but didn't set in. They sky continued to brighten, and as it did, we saw skeins of ducks passing back and forth over the pond. Some of them tilted toward our decoys, then continued on their way. Others turned for a closer look. A number of them set their wings and skidded in. They stayed long enough to figure out that the decoys were fakes before they wandered away.

In that half hour before legal shooting, we could have killed several limits apiece. "It's gonna be too easy," said Keith. "It's gonna be over before it starts. All that work for 10 minutes of shooting."

"Since when," I said, "did easy ever bother us?"

"I got an idea," he said. "Let's get our money's worth. Let's watch the birds fly for a while before we start shooting."

I liked that idea, so that's what we did. The air was full of ducks: blacks, mallards, woodies, teal, pintails, and redheads. We hunkered in our blind, drank coffee, and watched them fly while the sky brightened and the sun came up behind us and set the autumn foliage across the pond afire.

Finally Keith said, "We probably ought to shoot our ducks pretty soon."

I agreed. We loaded up, and Raisin, who knew what that meant, shivered.

And that's when the ducks stopped flying, of course. We sat there until 9:30, watching as the dawn turned into a bluebird October morning, and we never fired a shot. Then we shrugged, collected the decoys, took down the netting, piled everything into the canoe, paddled back across Tranquility, loaded Keith's truck, and went home.

We laughed about it. But we agreed that it had been a memorable Opening Day, and when we got to Keith's house and told his wife about all the ducks we'd seen, she said, "So you *don't* need to go hunting, shoot guns, and kill things to have fun, then?"

"You miss the point, sweetie," said Keith. "If we hadn't gone hunting, we wouldn't have been there in the first place."

Chapter 19

WILD PHEASANTS

I haven't even seen a wild pheasant in 20 years, much less shot one. A lot has changed since I was a kid growing up in a little farming community in eastern Massachusetts half a century ago.

Back then, there were pheasants in every field, oak ridge, swamp, and hedgerow. In the fall, after the cornfields had been cut, ringnecks prowled the brown stubble and jabbed at leftover kernels. In the winter they scuttled into our backyards to peck at the cracked corn and sunflower seeds that spilled from our birdfeeders.

Toward the end of August, as soon as the chicks had grown their flying feathers, we worked our bird dogs on wild pheasants. It was great pre-season practice for the dogs—not to mention a lot of fun for their handlers—to flush a covey of not-quite-grown pheasants over our setter's points and then chase down the singles.

It was also pre-season scouting, of course.

Everybody hunted wild pheasants in those days. They were our most popular, and most common, game bird, and on Opening Day, which in Massachusetts always fell on a Saturday, all of those fields and swales where we'd worked the dogs on broods of newly fledged pheasants swarmed with hunters.

My hunting pals and I did not compete with the mobs on Opening Day. We had our own tactic. In the northwest corner of town lay about 400 acres of field and swale—an area that was thick with pheasants, and well-known to local bird hunters. A little knobby hill covered with briar, scrubby oak, and stunted pine rose up in the middle of this expanse of pheasant cover. It looked like a green derby hat sitting on a big brown table.

We got up in the dark and were hiding on that hilltop a half hour before legal shooting on Opening Day. There we waited. About the time the sun peeked over the horizon, the armies of hunters began their invasion. From our observation site on the knoll, we could watch the dots of blaze-orange caps weave through the waist-high grass where, a month earlier, we'd worked our dogs. Soon we'd begin to hear distant shouts as ringnecks burst out of the fields, and we'd see the muzzle flashes and then hear the time-delayed volleys of shots as the birds flew the gauntlet.

Many of those pheasants headed straight for our ambush on the knoll. We always got our limits in the first hour or so of Opening Day.

After Opening Day, the mobs stopped coming, and we hunted pheasants the conventional way, criscrossing the fields with pointing bird dogs, and limits were hard to get.

Opening Day, I always believed, taught those crafty wild pheasants everything they needed to know about survival. They learned to run, not fly, and when they had to fly, they flaunted their size and speed. They burst up at the unexpected moment, cackling in panic, or derision. They were big birds, and their long tails made them seem twice as big as they were. They accelerated quicker and flew faster than they appeared to, and the tendency was to forget to lead them and shoot off their tails.

None of the farmers in my town had any problem with a couple of teenaged boys with shotguns prowling through their cornfields and hedgerows. Hunting was considered normal behavior when I was a kid. "Hunt anytime," those farmers always told us when we asked. "We got loads of pheasants."

Everything's different now. Mostly there are housing developments, condominiums, shopping malls, highway cloverleafs, and golf courses where the meadows, woodlots, and cornfields used to be. One by one, the old farmers yielded to the temptations of real-estate developers, and those who were left posted No Hunting signs around their properties. Sometimes, if you asked politely, they might give you permission to hunt, but most of them no longer trusted people with guns.

Many of the towns in the part of the world where I grew up have banned hunting entirely.

There aren't many wild pheasants left anyway. All those developments make poor pheasant habitat, and housecats, skunks, raccoons, crows, and hawks—creatures that are well-adapted to suburban civilization—prey efficiently on pheasant eggs and newly hatched chicks. It may be coincidence, but I trace the virtual disappearance of wild pheasants in eastern Massachusetts to the explosion in the coyote population over the past 20 or 30 years.

Today ringneck pheasants remain the most popular quarry for Massachusetts hunters, but the birds are no longer wild. They are raised in pens, and throughout the season they are released into the fifty-odd Wildlife Management Areas (our delightful euphemism for public hunting grounds) across the Commonwealth—the way hatchery trout are stocked in our ponds and streams—for the specific purpose of providing sport for licensed sportsmen.

Many of these WMAs offer classic pheasant habitat. The Division of Fisheries and Wildlife plants them with corn and millet, and they leave tangly edges and hedgerows. Many of the WMAs are bordered by boggy marshlands and swales, alder and poplar hillsides, and evergreen and oak forests. There's a science to the creation of pheasant habitat.

But if you've ever hunted wild pheasants, a WMA won't fool you. Armies of hunters have beaten permanent paths through the marshes and swales, and they leave empty 12-gauge shotgun shells scattered on the ground like confetti after a parade. There's always a lot of camaraderie on a WMA. Dogs sniff strange dogs, and hunters on the way out pass along rumors about how many birds were stocked that morning to the guys on the way in. The most important tactic for hunting success at a WMA is to get there early when there's still a space in the parking lot.

It's canned hunting. A WMA feels like an artificial trout pond, where you pay by the pound for the fish you catch. Pen-raised pheasants, like hatchery-raised brook trout, are not creatures of nature. They are not particularly cagey, swift, or smart. They are not survivors. They are raised to be "harvested," a wonderfully politically correct Fish and Wildlife euphemism that means "killed."

It's easy to shoot these pheasants without guilt. Their abundance, in fact, is directly proportional to the numbers of them that we kill. The more hunters who buy licenses and visit the WMAs, the more birds Fish and Wildlife can afford to raise and release for our hunting pleasure. They take surveys and use the results to lobby for their budgets. Pheasant hunting is politics these days.

I hunt them because if I want to go hunting for a few afternoon hours the way I used to when I was a kid, a WMA is all I've got amid the forests of No Hunting and No Trespassing signs.

I wouldn't think of visiting a WMA on a Saturday, but once in a while towards the end of a wet Thursday afternoon in November I find the parking lot at my local WMA empty. Burt and I work the thick edges where any pheasants that survived the morning's onslaught have likely taken cover. Stocked pheasants don't like to run the way their wild ancestors used to. They'll sit for a pointing dog. Burt likes that, and I do, too.

When I kick one of them up, it doesn't seem to fly as fast as I remember, either. I'm an average wingshot at best, but I rarely miss one of these lumbering domesticated birds.

Still, on those rare afternoons when dozens of bird dogs aren't crisscrossing every field and swale and when hunter-orange isn't the landscape's dominant color, I can sometimes delude myself into thinking that I'm hunting. After all, there are the birds, and there's the good cover, and I'm carrying a shotgun, and I've got my dog.

The delusion never lasts. It's *not* hunting, not really. It resembles hunting, but it's fake.

Southern quail hunters saw it coming a long time before we northern pheasant hunters did. Those of us who still prowl the uplands in the fall for ruffed grouse and wood-cock—truly wild birds — are doing our best to ignore the ticking clock.

Hunting on public land for stocked birds is the future, and we better get used to it.

This new version of pheasant hunting needs some fine-tuning. In its public forms such as the Massachusetts WMAs, there are too many hunters chasing too few birds over not enough acres of not very wild terrain.

Pheasant farmers, I understand, are now breeding hybrid birds, smaller, swifter fliers that give hunters a greater wingshooting challenge. This matters little to me. If the main point of hunting was target shooting, I'd give up flesh-and-blood birds entirely and shoot clays.

Every November, Art Currier, in celebration of his own birthday, organizes a day of pheasant hunting for himself and several of his old friends. Some of us have hunted and fished since we were kids. Others take to the woods only once a year, on Art's birthday hunt.

Because this is a special occasion, a once-a-year celebration of the season, we spend the day at a hunting preserve, sort of a private WMA, a northern version of a southern quail plantation, where we are assured of finding birds and privacy.

Over the years, we have sampled many New England pheasant preserves. We haven't found much difference among them. We pay a bird-per-man fee, which guarantees that a prescribed number of birds will be put out for us. On the morning of our arrival, one of the preserve's guides slips into our assigned fields and plants the pheasants, which have been rocked with their heads tucked under their wings so they will not fly or run away before we hunters get there.

Then we are divided into groups of three and directed to our appointed fields. We know six pheasants have been deposited there. If they are still there, and if our dogs do their jobs, we will get some shots and perhaps bag a few birds.

I always enjoy the comradeship of Art's day. I enjoy watching the dogs work, and shooting an occasional pen-reared pheasant does not give me the twinge of regret that I get when I shoot a wild bird.

We have the place to ourselves, we always find pheasants, the dogs point, and we knock birds out of the air. It's more fun than a WMA, but I never confuse a day on a preserve with wild-pheasant hunting. For that, I have to conjure up some old memories.

Chapter 20

LAST HUNT

Nick pulled his truck against the snowbank beside the mud-frozen road and turned off the engine. Last night's snow layered the dark hemlocks, and the scattering of old Baldwin apple trees on the hillside were black and gnarly. Here and there a wizened fruit still hung from a branch.

"Ah," said Nick's father from the seat beside him. "The Treacherous Owl. We had some fun here. I wondered where you were taking me."

"Looks different in the snow, huh?" said Nick.

"We never had any reason to come here in January," said the old man. "It was woodcock season when that owl showed us this place, wasn't it?"

Nick nodded. "October. The leaves hadn't dropped yet. That was a long time ago. I was just a kid, still trying to keep up with you in the woods."

They'd been driving the backroads that day, headed from one grouse cover to another one. Nick had been sitting in the passenger seat and his father was driving slowly, as he always did when they traveled the New Hampshire dirt roads. In the backseat, Duke, their old setter, had his chin on Nick's right shoulder and his nose poking out the open window. All three of them had their eyes peeled for road birds.

When the dark shadow glided across the roadway in front of them, Nick's father hit the brakes. "Did you see that?"

"What was it?" said Nick.

"Big old horned owl. Now what do you suppose he's up to?"

"Hunting," said Nick. "Like us."

"You suppose he knows something we don't know?"

"Bet he doesn't know the ten main exports of Bolivia," said Nick.

His father chuckled. "That knowledge wouldn't do him any more good than it'll do you. But I bet he knows where to find a good meal."

"You think he's hunting for grouse in there?"

"I think that I see alders, old apple trees, birch whips, and hemlocks, and I think I detect the ruts of an old cart path at that break in the stone wall," said the old man. "I bet we'll find a cellarhole in there where some old farmer made a nice grouse cover for us."

"We better take a look," said Nick.

His father backed up and pulled into the ancient roadway. Fifty yards in, at the top of a little round hill, they found the cellarhole. The farmhouse had collapsed into itself, but the fieldstone chimney still stood, and out back were a dozen toppled granite gravestones, so eroded by decades of wind and weather that Nick couldn't read the dates on them.

He hadn't yet begun carrying a gun in the woods in those days. His father called it his grouse-hunting apprenticeship. Nick had learned a lot, slogging through the woods behind his father, trying to match his old man's long-legged stride. He'd learned where grouse lived and how they flushed with a sudden explosion of wings, and he'd learned how his father's shotgun came up to his shoulder and began swinging at the sound before he saw anything.

When he thought about it, Nick realized he couldn't begin to enumerate the things he'd learned from trailing his father through the woods.

That owl had showed them a sweet little grouse cover. The apple orchard, which mingled with briar, juniper, thornapple, and patches of poplar, dribbled down the hill-side behind the cellarhole to a boggy little brook bordered by alders. Duke busted a couple of grouse as they worked their way through the orchard. Nick's old man yelled half-heartedly at the dog. They figured that, on balance, Duke did more good than harm, though it was a close call. The old setter never could figure out grouse, but he was death on wing-tipped birds and didn't mind pointing a wood-cock now and then.

When the dog locked on point in the alders, Nick's father handed the boy his shotgun. "Most likely a woodcock," the old man whispered. "When he flushes, take your time, let him get out there. Make sure you keep your head down. And don't forget the safety."

Nick nodded. His old man told him the same thing every time he let him try a shot. So far, Nick had never hit a flying bird of any kind. His father always said, "Tough shot" or "That bird zigged when he should've zagged" or "I thought you were right on him," as though he actually expected the boy to connect. "The law of averages will catch up with you," his father would say. "When it does, watch out birds." Personally, Nick wondered if he'd ever hit anything.

When woodcock flushed in thick alders, Nick had observed that the birds tended to helicopter straight up and kind of hang there for a minute before they darted off in some unpredictable direction. But this time, when Nick walked up behind Duke and the bird took flight, it stayed low. Nick's gun came up to his shoulder and his thumb flicked off the safety and he remembered to snuggle his cheek against the stock, but the way the bird was weaving back and forth through the alders, Nick couldn't get on him.

His old man always said, "You can't kill anything you don't shoot at," so just as the bird was about to disappear out of range, Nick pulled the trigger.

"Hey," his old man yelled. "You got him." Nick could hear how he was trying not to sound surprised.

A minute later Duke came back with the dead woodcock in his mouth. Nick's father said, "Thank you," and took the bird from the dog. He held it in his hand and stroked its head with his forefinger. "A lovely little bird," he said softly. "Sometimes I wish we could put them back, like trout." He handed the woodcock to Nick. "Congratulations. Good shooting."

"Thank you, law of averages," Nick said on that October day more than 40 years ago when the horned owl flew across the road.

"Look how tall those beeches are now," Nick's old man said as they sat there in the truck looking out at the snowy January landscape. "The Treacherous Owl's way past its prime."

Nick found himself smiling. "Aren't we all."

"We packed away a lot of memories here, though, didn't we?"

Nick nodded. "That's why I thought this was where we should come today. To remember. My Bucky pup made his first point right in there." Nick pointed into the woods.

They both looked out the window of the truck. "That was a lovely sidehill of birch whips when we first started coming here," said the old man. "Not much taller than a man's head. There was always a woodcock or two in those birches. Look at 'em now."

Now they were grown-up trees as thick through the trunk as a strong man's arm.

"Bucky was what, 6 months old that season?" said Nick's father. "Tiny little thing. All ears and enthusiasm."

"Right," said Nick. "The birches had grown a little taller by then, but it was still a good spot for woodcock. That was the only time I remember feeling as though I absolutely had to shoot a bird. To reward Bucky for his point."

Nick's father chuckled quietly, and Nick understood that he was remembering what Nick was remembering. Bucky had skidded into a point in the middle of the birches, and Nick had pushed in, flushed the woodcock, and missed it with both barrels, and then his father had shot once and dumped the bird. The old man had always been a better wingshot than Nick, even at the very end of his shooting days. He had never once gloated about it.

When that woodcock dropped amid the birches, Bucky had toddled over to it, sniffed at it, then put his paw on it and stood there proudly. Nick had never been able to persuade Bucky to retrieve woodcock.

"This was the place where you quit hunting for good," Nick said after a few minutes. "It was the last cover you carried a gun in."

"I don't remember it that way," said the old man.

"I do," said Nick.

It was one of those gray November afternoons, Nick recalled, 20 or 25 years after the day the owl had flown across the road. Bucky was an old dog by then. He'd slowed down a lot, and he'd finally begun to point grouse fairly regularly. So when he locked on a point in a brushy corner on the edge of the old pasture, Nick and his father had moved up quickly on either side of the dog.

The grouse flushed on the old man's side, and instead of darting through the thick stuff and heading for the distant stand of pines, the way any self-respecting grouse would do, this one chose to fly across the open field. Nick watched his father's gun come up and swing on the bird, and in his head he uttered a little benediction for the doomed grouse. The old man never missed an easy crossing shot.

"Bang-bang," Nick's father had said conversationally.

The bird kept flying.

The old man lowered his gun, blew imaginary smoke away from its barrels, and grinned at Nick. "Got him."

"Huh?" said Nick. "You didn't even shoot at him. What happened?"

"Safety stuck."

Nick rolled his eyes. "That's a damn lie."

The old man smiled, then nodded and tapped his forehead with his fingertip. "Got him here, in my imagination. Then I put him back, like a trout." He shrugged. "I've killed an awful lot of birds. More than my share, I figure. One more or less doesn't matter to me. Now we know he's still here."

"What're you trying to say?" said Nick.

The old man dismissed the subject with a flip of his hand. "Nothing very profound."

Bucky died the following spring, and Nick was in no hurry to replace him. When the bird season rolled around, Nick's father kept turning down invitations to hunt with other men's dogs. Nick didn't push him. Grouse hunting wasn't the same without your own dog.

That winter the old man gave Nick his 50-year-old Winchester Model 21, the only gun he'd ever carried in grouse cover. "It's the arthritis," he said. "I just can't get around the way I used to."

Nick didn't believe that. But he knew his old man too well, and respected him too much, to argue with him.

They sat there in the front seat of the truck, looking out the window at the way the cold afternoon sunlight angled in through the trees, not saying anything. Nick, for one, was in no hurry to get on with it, and he guessed his old man was feeling the same.

Nick's mind was whirling with memories. "That time you said 'bang-bang' to the grouse wasn't the last time we came here together," he said finally.

"I remember," the old man said quietly. "You talked me into it."

"I wanted you to see Burt work." Burt was Nick's new Brittany, barely 8 months old that fall, but already pointing woodcock like a veteran. "You finally agreed to walk through one cover with me. We came here."

"Burt was a precocious bird dog, all right," said the old man. "The cover had grown up and gone to hell by then, though. It was sad to see. Made me feel old."

Nick smiled. "You *were* old."

They'd made a short hunt of it. The only part of the Treacherous Owl cover that looked any good was the alder run, and anyway, Nick's father was pretty hobbled with his arthritis. Nick carried the old Winchester Model 21, Burt darted and pranced ahead of him on his short puppy legs, and the old man limped along behind. Nick tried to keep his pace slower than normal, and every now and then he looked back over his shoulder and said, "How you doin'?"

"I can still keep up with the likes of you," the old man answered.

Burt pointed the only woodcock they found in the Treacherous Owl that day, and Nick missed it with both barrels.

"He zigged when he should've zagged," the old man said, still making excuses for him.

Now Nick gazed out at the snowy landscape and said, "That day I brought you here to see Burt work—did it remind you of anything?"

"Oh," his father said, "it reminded me of a whole life-time of things."

"I mean, you following behind me, trying to keep up," Nick said. "Me carrying the Model 21. Me being the one who yelled at the dog."

Nick's father was quiet for a long time. Then he said, "Full circle, huh? I was the kid that day, and you were the father."

"No," said Nick. "You've always been the father."

"Well," Nick's old man said a few minutes later, "we going to sit here all day?"

"I guess it's time," Nick said.

They got out of the truck and crunched through the crusty ankle-deep snow on the old woodsroad to the cellarhole on the hilltop. A big old hemlock—it probably had been a sapling that day 40-odd years ago when the owl flew across the road—grew behind the garden of toppled gravestones, and under its lowermost boughs the earth was bare. The afternoon January sun came streaming in, and from the top of the hill you could see over the treetops to some distant New Hampshire mountains.

"This okay?" said Nick.

"This is perfect," said the old man.

Nick knelt down and spread his father's ashes under the hemlock boughs. He thought he should probably say something, but he couldn't think of anything that had been left unsaid between them. They'd finally and truly come full circle, and that was that.